T0277120

Cambridge Elements ≡

Elements in Applied Linguistics
edited by
Li Wei
University College London
Zhu Hua
University College London

WRITING BANAL INEQUALITIES

How to Fabricate Stories That Disrupt

Edited by

Hannah Cowan
King's College London

Alfonso Del Percio
University College London

CAMBRIDGE
UNIVERSITY PRESS

Shaftesbury Road, Cambridge CB2 8EA, United Kingdom

One Liberty Plaza, 20th Floor, New York, NY 10006, USA

477 Williamstown Road, Port Melbourne, VIC 3207, Australia

314–321, 3rd Floor, Plot 3, Splendor Forum, Jasola District Centre,
New Delhi – 110025, India

103 Penang Road, #05–06/07, Visioncrest Commercial, Singapore 238467

Cambridge University Press is part of Cambridge University Press & Assessment,
a department of the University of Cambridge.

We share the University's mission to contribute to society through the pursuit of
education, learning and research at the highest international levels of excellence.

www.cambridge.org
Information on this title: www.cambridge.org/9781009108515

DOI: 10.1017/9781009104449

First published 2023

A catalogue record for this publication is available from the British Library.

ISBN 978-1-009-10851-5 Paperback
ISSN 2633-5069 (online)
ISSN 2633-5050 (print)

Cambridge University Press & Assessment has no responsibility for the persistence
or accuracy of URLs for external or third-party internet websites referred to in this
publication and does not guarantee that any content on such websites is, or will
remain, accurate or appropriate.

Writing Banal Inequalities

How to Fabricate Stories that Disrupt

Elements in Applied Linguistics

DOI: 10.1017/9781009104449
First published online: May 2023

Hannah Cowan
King's College London

Alfonso Del Percio
University College London

Author for correspondence: Hannah Cowan, Hannah.Cowan@kcl.ac.uk

Abstract: In this Element, the authors write about the everyday production and experiences of banal inequality. Through a series of sections, each comprising a blog post written for *Disruptive Inequalities* and a commentary from the author on the predicaments they encountered in the writing process, this Element shares, and confronts, the ways we fabricate stories and use writing to resist. It makes visible the choices, practices, and reflections that have led to the writing of our stories and offers the tools we have used to fabricate them to all those who may find them meaningful to appropriate, adapt, and translate to fight the struggles that they want to fight. These tools are formulated in a way for writers to develop their own methods of storytelling and activism. the authors hope this Element contributes to an ongoing debate on how writing serves banal resistance.

Keywords: writing, ethnography, inequality, disruption, activism

ISBNs: 9781009108515 (PB), 9781009104449 (OC)
ISSNs: 2633-5069 (online), 2633-5050 (print)

Contents

1 Introduction: Writing Banal Inequalities by Alfonso Del Percio and Hannah Cowan

In this Element, we advance a form of ethnographic writing which allows us to spotlight, denormalise, and attempt to disrupt the everyday ordinariness of people's unequal experience of comfort, wealth, and power in the present; what we call *banal inequality*. Building on Hannah Arendt's (1963) conceptualisation of the *Banality of Evil* and Michael Billig's (1995) notion of *Banal Nationalism*, we are interested in how writing can allow us to fabricate and circulate stories that analyse, make visible, circulate, and possibly transform the modes of thinking, habits, and daily practices that allow inequality to be perceived as a normal characteristic of our daily life. Along with Arendt and Billig, we think that social inequality is neither an anomaly nor a foreign body which is imposed from outside onto groups of people. Nor is inequality something that we can locate at the social and political peripheries of the worlds we inhabit. Inequality, we think, is an intrinsic, constitutive, and normalised part of the social. It manifests in the people, things, and relations that we live with.

Foregrounding the banal nature of inequality does not mean that we consider it benign, harmless, or innocent. Rather, it is a way for us to point to the routinisation of inequality in the social fabric. It is routinised because it is encapsulated in daily depersonalised, mundane, and normalised everyday activities and remains often unnoticed and unspoken, sometimes considered as standard, especially by those contributing to its perpetuation. Inspired by Arendt's analysis of the mundane manifestations of evil, which she suggests led to and normalised the Holocaust during World War Two, we claim that inequality is rarely produced by those who are 'sadistic', 'perverse', or 'demonic', but through the terrible normality of mundane habits. Drawing on Billig's understanding of nationalism as an endemic condition of Western nation states, we argue that banal inequality is powerful because it has entered a symbiotic relationship with many societies in which we live. It is seen by those actors who hold power as an integral part of a normalised, natural, biological order – the difference between men and women, the existence and superiority of certain races, the survival of the fittest, the natural laws of the market – that is said to constitute society and therefore is necessary to keep society healthy and allow it to evolve. At the same time, inequality is often justified as the logical and natural consequence of normalised social and cultural regimes and moral norms that a society expresses. Writing banal inequality means for us to produce stories which not only challenge these normalised, hegemonic, and, we would argue, harmful narratives of the social, but to produce alternative, more complex, and sometimes contradictory, accounts of inequality which open new possibilities for transformation.

This Element, then, is an attempt to intervene in a larger social and political debate amongst academics and political activists about what it means to write inequality. While this project began in an online blog called *Disruptive Inequalities*, here we benefit from the affordances provided by this Element, and work with some of the contributors we have collaborated with over the last six years to open the black box of our own writing practices about banal inequality. Through a series of sections, each comprising a blog post which has been written for *Disruptive Inequalities* and a commentary from the author on the predicaments they encountered in the writing process, we intend to make visible what often remains hidden in the textual products that make it onto library shelves; namely, the choices, strategies, practices, and reflections that have led to the writing of our stories of banal inequality. In doing so we offer our stories of banal inequality, and the tools we have used to fabricate them, to all those who may find them meaningful to appropriate, adapt, and translate to fight the struggles that they want to fight. These tools are not quick-fix flat-pack components; rather, they are a set of predicaments for writers to think with to develop their own methods of storytelling. Indeed, we hope this Element is just a beginning – that it provokes a debate on how we can use our writing to disrupt banal inequalities.

1.1 Writing the Microphysics of Inequality

We all write from our own standpoint, from our own sense of urgency and hope, and the impetus to contribute to the imagination and enactment of a different world. While we believe crisis to have been a perpetual state of being over centuries, the texts presented in this Element are situated in each author's own iterations of crises: the Covid-19 pandemic, nationalism, state violence, and economic oppression. Our texts have also been inspired, framed, and shaped for example by climate change, Shaheen Bagh, LGBTQ+, Black Lives Matter activists, as well as feminist, socialist, and anarchist writers who mobilise old and develop new forms of expression to challenge and transform the multiple forms of social inequality that this sense of perpetual crisis has contributed to normalise. These sources of inspiration do not necessarily build a comprehensive theorisation of the social to draw upon, nor do they offer a coherent utopian project around which different political struggles can be organised. They represent different political histories, and are scattered, often incomplete (i.e., made and remade), and sometimes conflicting, political projects which however converge in their joint struggle in favour of a more equal and just world. Similarly, our own divergent personal trajectories, our different experiences, make it that as authors and editors of this Element, we tend to ask different questions and develop diverging, and sometimes even conflicting, understandings of the harms we witness. We decided not to erase our multiple standpoints, since this would have meant invisiblising our personal histories, the reasons for which we came to engage in this publication project. Our own struggles and fights. At the same time, we did not want our divergent points of view to divide us. Transformation has to be collective. Therefore, we chose to join forces around our common interest in banal inequality and around the idea that writing can provide us with forms of power that allow us to undo and disrupt inequality. If, as Arendt suggests, banal actions can produce something as evil and spectacular as genocide, then, we think it may be possible for our banal writing practices to cause spectacular disruptions. We call this mode of writing banal inequalities which we advocate in this Element 'microphysical writing'.

Through this Element, then, we seek to shape alliances with all these political writers who, along with other forms of political actions such as boycotts, strikes, blockades, sabotage, and sit-ins, produce and circulate texts to propagate a different mode of looking at and speaking about the social worlds we inhabit, including alternative modes of being society. Our intervention consists of a set of reflections about how specific modes of microphysical ethnographic writing allow us not just to put the spotlight on the normalised practices that shape inequality, but also enable us to identify moments of transformation. We argue that too many politically orientated social scientists and activist scholars have understood these processes of inequality by pointing to big, spectacular, yet ephemeral processes, neglecting their everyday unfolding and social effects. For Hannah, terms such as austerity, neoliberalism, and even capitalism have become in danger of being used as a silver bullet to plug every rebellious query as an explanation for evil, even when people are using the term to mean different things (Bell & Green, 2016). These isms, much like fascism in Arendt's time, often get spoken about as big co-optive evils, such as when Latour (2005) mocks the invisible forces or discourses that seem to mysteriously infiltrate our ways of life. With Callon (1998), she claims that people (and things) are made up of all the other people and things they have interacted with throughout their lives. Our selves, our beings, are made up of our relations.

Alfonso, however, thinks that our everyday practices, modes of thinking, costumes, our habits, bodies, and affect are inextricably interwoven with the macro-relations of the political/economic/social systems in place, including the tools, cultural principles, and forms of knowledge through which they operate. He thinks that categories such as capitalism and colonialism, including the forms of racism, classism, sexism, and homophobia they produce, can be useful since they allow us to collectivise inequality. Collectivising means for Alfonso that experiences of inequality are always linked with forms of inequality happening in other places, at another moment in time. This also means for him that these mundane experiences are interwoven with people's and institutions' attempts to perpetuate inequality, to manage and regulate it, and in certain cases to benefit from it. Writing the microphysics of inequality is then for Alfonso a powerful way to connect the intimate, mundane, and the everyday to what happens elsewhere and to account for the dialectic relation between the complex, fractured, and sometimes contradictory histories of capitalism and colonialism and the multiple, fluctuating, and intersectional positions that can lead to social exclusion, violence, and oppression (Crenshaw, 2015; Lakshmi Peipzna-Samarasinha, 2018).

Hannah is more cautious. Rather than only seeing the macro enfolded into and reinforced by the micro, for her the macro is nothing more than what exists and gets produced in the everyday materialities of life – people, animals, goods, food, things – and the practices and relations between them that produce various levels of comfort. Consequently, she claims, we need to write and circulate stories that account for the relations between different people, communities, and the material world, including goods, food, comfort, and all these things that we consider to be essential to live the life we would like to live – and this is how intersectionality manifests.

Despite these theoretical differences, we converge in the conviction that there is a need for a mode of writing that does not take inequality for granted, but that stresses with precision how, when, where, by whom, and with what effects inequality comes to be produced, normalised, and banalised; how it affects real people in their real lives. This we call microphysical writing. We also agree that this means producing stories that account for the shifting, often unexpected, dynamics between the oppressor and oppressed. Stories that help us clarify the specific circumstances, practices, different spaces, relations, logics, or periods of time under and through which harm and oppression are produced. This, we think, allows us to provide nuance to nostalgic accounts that understand inequality as the product of class relations, the stigmatised racial other, or the dominated gendered self that tend to put people into neat boxes, recreating solidified categories of people which have themselves caused so much harm (Mehan, Hertweck, & Meihls, 1986; McKittrick, 2021).

1.2 Fabricating Stories

Attending to and transforming banal inequality through microphysical writing, telling complex and sometimes seemingly contradictory stories that challenge hegemonic and highly normalising accounts of inequality, means for us that we need to think about the ways we fabricate and tell these complex stories. The words we place on the page are the product of a crafting process which shapes and artificially stabilises the world, our practices, and relations. And this is not only because the picture we produce of the forms of violence, dispossession, and oppression that we write often tends to erase our doubts, questions, and partial, precarious, and fluctuating understanding of things. It is because there is no single truth of how the world *is* to report on in the first place. As Law and Lien (2012) explain, scientific textbook definitions attempting to depict a stable universal classification of the world (including an account of banal inequality) end up locating it in a strange immaterial white space with little relation to what various people, things, and animals *do* to make themselves and the world around them. These relations and practices that make us up are multiple, meaning that every form of knowledge, academic or not, whether, like some forms of statistics, it claims to depict a singular truth about the world, can only ever be a story or a partial one-sided truth about the world. As Will sets out in the very first section of this Element, our stories are always a patchwork of things we've seen or come to know through other stories, whether we are writing a fictional fantasy or about the world we dwell in. We are constantly treading the precipice between fact and fiction – stories can even get incorporated into our very bodies and identity. This relativity does not mean we can be complacent about which story we choose to tell. As Amal argues in her contribution, our stories do something, act upon the world, upon our readers and ourselves – they hold power. And as we construct the world through our stories, we make important choices – we take sides.

We make choices about what and whose stories we want to tell. What raw materials do we draw on, what doors do we go through, what spaces do we visit? Who or what do we pay attention to in the room? Do we look for practices, experiences, emotions, or interactions? Then we move on to the millions of decisions and indecisions in how we choose to assemble our stories. Fabricating stories requires us to make choices – to highlight or select some aspects of the story while erasing others. How do we weave together the actors? How do we run, catch, or cross them together in the various ways we choose to describe the speech or movements of our interlocutors and the spaces we find or suggest for resistance? Also, how do we account for the messy and often contradictory stories about banal inequality that we want to tell? If we stay with Hannah Arendt for a moment, how can we write a story about this key figure in Western political thinking that considers both her critique of Nazi totalitarianism and at the same time her blindness for the sociopolitical significance of race and racism in the West, especially her advocacy for racial school segregation in the American South? As Natassia's story teaches us, denaturalising inequality means resisting the imperative of order and simplification that informs many writings in the social sciences. We chose to rather embrace the routinised, but also dynamic, fluctuating, and often unexpected practices, relations, associations, links, and logics, as well as structures, materials, and affect that constitute banal inequality. We reject ready-made stories about inequality, in which the plot is organised around standardised, socially shared, and accepted models of portraying oppressor/oppressed relations. We think that more than illuminating the manifestations and effects of inequality, such standardised stories contribute to the naturalisation of inequality.

Making choices also means for us to choose a language, a mode of writing our stories of banal inequality which allows us to be understood by the publics we interact with. Many political writers, especially academics, are used to telling their stories in a way that makes them often difficult to be understood by their readers. This is how we, as academics, are used to building authority (Bourdieu, 1984). Language is a social practice that can give some of us authority and prestige. The enactment of abstract, heavily theoretical, forms of writing gives us authority because they create the illusion of objectivity and disinterest – stories written from nowhere (Bauman & Briggs, 2004). We believe this is a problem because this mode of writing relies on a long history of academic expertise tangled up in patriarchy (rich man knows best) and colonial politics (Europeans going round the world to categorise everyone and everything and call it fact) (Heller & McElhinny, 2017). As Sibo argues in his text, we need a different language to talk about the inequalities and the violence, domination, and oppression around us. In writing the microphysics of banal inequalities, along with the relations that everyone is invited to interpret, we aim to operate on a different notion of authority. Let's be clear, we are convinced that all stories are fabricated, and that gives the author power and control over how the story gets told. We also reject the idea of having to mirror, in our writing, our readers' imagined way of speaking and writing. We think that this is infantilising and reproduces the patriarchal assumptions that we intend to challenge. However, we want readers to be able to see where we are, who we are, and the relations we observe that led to us to making our claims. We also want our doubts and changes in terms of how we see things to be expressed and discussed explicitly. We therefore chose to avoid incomprehensible and unnecessary jargon that obfuscates, rather than clarifies, the dynamics constituting banal inequality, so that, as Natassia argues, our readers can engage with and critique our stories, thinking about how they might have written them differently.

Choosing a language that engages our readers also involves us asking questions about how we construct plots and storylines. Will argues that writing stories includes strategically choosing a genre, that is, socially accepted ways of telling a story about banal inequality that can be heard, that convinces, that allows us to convene the argument that we want our texts to circulate. Powerful stories (about banal inequality), Will notes, are not necessarily those which reproduce the social and literary orders which inform genre conventions (standardised modes of organising stories and speech more generally (Briggs & Bauman, 1992)), but quite to the contrary those which play with or subvert genre expectations, those that tell the social differently. With Will, we argue for stories that subvert genre expectations not only because of their unexpected, creative, aesthetic, and playful effects, but because this stylistic strategy allows us to replace hegemonic ways of writing, understanding, and explaining inequality with modes of telling and writing which denormalise and denaturalise inequality, which propagate alternative stories about inequality and open up possibilities for transformation.

Reflecting genres also requires us to choose how to write ourselves in the stories we fabricate. For us this is not just a stylistic move, not one possibility amongst others, but an act of intellectual rigour and political transparency. We are convinced that we are part of the weave of the stories we fabricate. For sure, our stories are contingent on what we know about the social worlds we inhabit; the stories we write are stories we witness. There are stories we can't tell because we have not experienced them, felt them, engaged with them, and those we feel compelled to tell because we have. But we also argue that there is a need for us to make our choices explicit, to explain from where (geographically, politically, socially) we are speaking. This is not simply to advocate the imperative of reflexivity – to reflect on our own assumptions and judgements – which has become mainstream in ethnographic writing (Bourdieu, 2007). We want to go further by writing ourselves into the story and developing an account of banal inequality that collapses the distance between the author and the world the author is enunciating, giving shape to. While we are inspired by autoethnographic methods, a practice which according to Adams, Jones, and Ellis (2014) allows us to know, name, and interpret personal and cultural experience, in this Element we follow Abu Lughod's (2008) demand for a constant problematisation of the power exerted by us, both as writers and as members of the societies which we document. This means offering a mode of writing that reveals the ways in which we as writers are always a subject and protagonist of our stories: not for the pleasure of centralising our selves, but because we think we are involved in the relations of oppression and domination that we report.

All these choices encapsulate a maybe more fundamental point. Writing means us taking sides. Our writing is always political; it always takes sides – and so we must decide what matters to us at a specific moment in time. This certainly is not wholly a rational endeavour, but one which requires emotion.

As Hannah suggests in Section 7, we must sometimes let anger guide the decisions in our writing; our stories are both shaped by passion and at the same time are intended to shape passion. This is not to say this is an individualistic process – our affects are shared; this is politics. Our stories are written in a way to affect, touch, move, overwhelm, mobilise. We must therefore consider the concerns of the audiences we write for; the stories we tell are meant to intervene in the public debate and shape alliances or provocations with other stories told by other people conducting the same or different fights. Along with Sibo, we are convinced that writing about banal inequality is rioting. Our stories don't reassure; they overwhelm, attack the dynamics of inequality where they have effects on people, they provoke disruption and, as Amal explains, transformation.

1.3 Commonising Knowledge Production

This Element is an attempt to 'commonise' knowledge production (Caffentzis & Federici, 2014) and to contribute to the collective capacity to tell stories about inequality differently, in a multitude of contradictory ways, with new plots, new rhythms, new locations, and new modes of portraying the oppressive worlds surrounding us. We have already seen some attempts to commonise knowledge, but these have all too often been about democratising the consumption of knowledge rather than its production – about reading rather than writing. The Reformation, the printing press, the libraries we see in so many towns and cities; they are all about spreading the word – whether of god or of powerful thinkers educated in particular, often homogenised, fashions. This supposed democratisation of knowledge has been shown to serve traditional forms of power, agendas of the state and capital through the instilment of cultural values into people's minds (Gramsci, 1971). Using democracy to think about knowledge forces us to choose one form of knowledge over another and to constantly suppress alternative ideas, priorities, and choices (Graeber, 2004). In this Element, we therefore focus on writing instead of reading, drawing on Caffentzis and Federici's (2014) work on building a collective practice of commoning, which we understand as a way to reclaim control over the conditions of knowledge production, and knowledge on banal inequality in particular. We join Caffentzis and Federici (2014) in contributing to what they call a 'common wealth' (p. 101), a concept which should not be confused with *the Commonwealth*, which is the neo-imperial project put in place by the British state to maintain its influence over former territories of the British Empire. Along with Caffentzis and Federici, we rather understand 'common wealth' as a shared system of knowledge and communication which allows us to disentangle our lives from the market and the state, reclaim our collective understanding and memory of the unequal and oppressive worlds we have had to (and continue to) inhabit, and identify alternatives to the present.

Let's be clear. Attempting to commonise knowledge production does not mean that everybody can tell and write their stories. Writing remains a privilege for all those of us who are not fully absorbed by the precarity of our lives, reproductive work, and the necessity to satisfy our basic needs and the needs of those for whom we care. And let's not forget that writing, especially political writing, is often subjected to surveillance, violence, and control, so that all writers are not free to propagate their stories. Also, not all forms of writing are seen as equally valuable. Writing is itself a practice around which inequality is organised. Some forms of writing are considered as more correct, more analytical, more beautiful, and more powerful than others. And while writing in any language comes with socially shared expectations about how stories need to be told, we are aware that writing in English, the language of the global academic elite, creates its own particular social hierarchies, inequalities, and exclusions. We are not external to these processes. In making our blog and this Element, we are always in danger of reproducing these normalised ideas about writing. We act as gatekeepers, deciding whose stories we want to publish, and whose we do not. We think that not all stories should be told and circulated. Some stories are harmful and contribute to the reproduction of the forms of inequality we contest and intend to transform. The line between commonising writing and subjecting writers to control, stigma, and discipline has always been fine. Finding this balance has meant for us to never romanticise our practice of commonising, to never neglect the implications of our choices and decisions, and to keep looking for modes of solidarity which allow us to handle and rebalance power, including the power to decide what counts as a good story, what counts as a good text, and who counts as a good writer. Opening the black box of our writing practice is a first step for us in this direction. It is a way to share our reflections, strategies, and methods, adding to the growing common wealth of political tactics, tools, strategies, and writings which is inspiring and informing collective action and intersectional alliances in many parts of the world.

The word now goes to our contributors and their sections.

You are welcome to pick each section out on its own, paired with its blog post, but we have ordered the sections as such to start with the way we construct the narrative as a whole, then to think about the detail in our stories, before moving on to how we find space for our stories to disrupt the banal inequalities we document. Will begins in Section 2 with his conviction that 'everything is genre' or at least gets genred. A good story, he suggests, never conforms to the genres people expect, but works against it. We then go on to Natassia in Section 3, who suggests we embrace the complexity in our stories, and work to materialise it and hold it 'in place' for our readers to participate in the storytelling. In Section 4, Alfonso thinks about the aesthetics of oppression in our writing and how we must complicate the usual dichotomy of oppressor–oppressed relations. Amal takes the first steps in Section 5 towards thinking more concretely about how our writing can disrupt inequalities through documenting and writing oppression. In doing so, she comes up against the issue of how we write our oppressors, and how at times kindness is needed to understand the banal. In Section 6, Sibo continues this move to the question of 'what can be done?' by thinking of writing as rioting. We can use it not only to speak out, but to speak in ways which subvert the linguistic apparatus of oppression. Finally, in Section 7 Hannah explores how writing can be a way to utilise anger and locate places to disrupt in our everyday actions. In the Conclusion we develop these ideas on how the practice of writing banal inequalities can, under specific conditions, lead to more mundane, but potentially more effective, forms of resistance.

2 Everything Is Genre by Will Nyerere Plastow

2.1 Blog Post

POSTED 9 FEBRUARY 2018

Thieving Black Man(liness): When Cultural Appropriation Becomes Entirely Necessary

Figure 2.1 'Erislandy Lara vs. Carlos Molina at Fight Night at The Cosmopolitan of Las Vegas' by The Cosmopolitan of Las Vegas, 2011. Licensed under CC BY-ND 2.0.

I stepped out of the ring, my brain aching and my mouth tasting of blood. For the final round I'd had tunnel vision, trying to beat down my rapidly tiring opponent. But I hadn't done enough. I had lost.

As I walked to my changing room, a professional boxer from the audience stopped me to talk. 'Don't get down, you took a huge shot in the first. Most would have given up there but you fought through. He was almost gone at the end. You've got the heart to go pro with this, all the lads were saying.'

I still probably think about this small moment of recognition at least once a week.

I was brought up by my posh white single mum, in a lower middle-class suburb of Leeds. I was one of about ten non-white kids in a high school of fifteen hundred. The dickheads at school soon made clear what was wrong with me; I was too posh, not manly enough, and not sufficiently black (for my appearance).

The message was clear. I had to become less posh, manlier, and blacker. To me, all these things were clearly linked. A half millennium of racist mythologising means they're probably linked for you too. Think about the words Black Man and let an image form in your mind. Is it posh? Or at some deep level do you code that working class is manlier than posh, that black is more hypermasculine than white?

My problem was that I was posh, I hardly knew any adult men, and I literally knew no black people my age. As you might have guessed by this point, my Tanzanian dad wasn't exactly a big part of my childhood. If I wanted to become someone manly and black, and therefore in my mind the opposite of posh, I was going to have to improvise.

We usually talk about cultural appropriation as something big, and something bad. It's black and white minstrel shows, it's the Washington Redskins refusing to change their name, it's Scarlett Johanssen playing a character called Matoko Kusananji. Cultural appropriation is an idea that is very useful when we see someone powerful messing around with the culture of someone less powerful and we want to say, 'that's fucked up'. It's also an idea I've got some pretty big problems with. Because when you don't know any black men and want to (are inevitably going to) become a black man, you're going to have to appropriate.

A truly frightening amount of who I am has come, consciously or unconsciously, from films and music. This ranges from the innocent; buying Hip Hop CDs with my pocket money and studiously checking the words I didn't know on *Urban Dictionary* so I could use them myself, to the not so innocent; like the deep-founded belief in the connection between the capacity for violence and manliness that I will never be rid of. One trait I picked up that caused my friends endless amusement was my 'black voice'.

> *'Ayiiit girl, what's happening yeah? Me I just been chillin with my girl cousin innit.'*

My 'black voice' was how I spoke to my few black acquaintances at sixth form. It used to make my close (white) friends laugh when I switched my accent from one moment to the next. My black acquaintances didn't laugh, even when my 'black voice' was (see above) pretty unconvincing. I guess they must have seen me as another black person. If I said some dumb stuff sometimes, and I did, it wasn't dumb enough to be all that interesting.

My point is that a large part of who I am comes from me appropriating other people's cultures. This isn't an innocent process. The people whose lives I mined to recreate myself as someone masculine and black were overwhelmingly poorer, blacker people than myself. My cultural appropriation was as much about class as about race. With poshness and effeminacy linked in my mind, I wanted to steal a bit of macho glamour from people who really faced danger in their day to day lives. At different times in my life, I tried a pretty wide range of strategies to do this, from taking up boxing and training at an inner-city gym, to practising saying 'motherfucker' in the mirror until it sounded natural enough to use in casual conversation.

This is my problem with the idea of cultural appropriation . . .

> 'Appropriate – Take (something) for one's own use, typically without the owner's permission.' (*Oxford English Dictionary*)

To appropriate culture, culture has to become a *thing*, that can be owned. For culture to have owners there must be a core group of people who are the authentic bearers of that culture, either because they made it, or have a long term personal or family connection with it. But this vision, where an in-group of authentic culture-owners must protect their culture from outsiders who want to steal or undermine it, has always felt, to me, very close to nationalism – something else I don't really understand.

If you don't really fit in where you grow up, and mixed race people are the misfits par excellence, you notice the work it takes to belong anywhere. Despite my presumably equal mix of genetic material from my mum and dad, in the UK people are more likely to categorise me as black/other rather than white/same. Since childhood, I've travelled around East Africa quite a lot. It was pretty sobering when I got old enough to realise that there most people see me as *Mizungu* – white/other.

We are born into a place in society, but we are not born with identities – crying, drinking milk, and not being able to sit up does not count as an identity. Identities have to be created, borrowing bits from the people we encounter both in real life and in fiction, and then redrafting ourselves to accommodate these new bits until hopefully we create someone we can live with being.

These days I spend a lot of my spare time on (hopefully) creative writing. This has made me think a lot about the similarities between the ways in which we create ourselves and writing a story. The basic parameters are set before you begin, there will be a beginning, middle, and an end, with a central character who will (hopefully) learn something over the course of events. The creativity comes in how you fulfil this basic outline, and, to a large degree, the way you fulfil it is by stealing other people's ideas. The skill is adjusting these ideas to your purposes and bolting them back together in a way that is hopefully too subtle for anybody to see the joins. If you're really, really good at it, you might even create a tiny sliver of something original as you go along.

If you think I'm just saying this because I'm a hack, it's worth remembering nearly all Shakespeare's plays are re-writes of pre-existing stories. So even if I personally am a hack, I'm in good company here.

Gender, race, and class are identities that are often violently imposed on people from the outside, but they are also identities that we creatively improvise and project outwards. I am about the millionth person to the party to say identities are performances. For a huge number of people, especially people who, for whatever reason, struggled to fit into the local culture they grew up in, some of the elements of that performance are going to be stolen. And sometimes that can give people space to express themselves and create things which are brilliant ...

Figure 2.2 Freddie Mercury. The most famous Tanzanian–Briton mix and man who borrowed ideas from everywhere and made them awesome.

And sometimes not so much . . .

Figure 2.3 Musical artist 'Vanilla Ice' by wonker (2010). Licensed under CC BY 2.0.

2.2 Commentary

'What you got for me?'
Sound clever, sound clever, says the voice inside my head. At least come up with
   something.

'Eight by thirty min action comedy with black teen leads', I begin.

Wait, that isn't right. I'm not talking to a TV producer. It's my mate Hannah on the other end of the line. She wants my essay idea for the Element she's editing. Really gotta sound clever. Academic clever.

I burble something about being a screenwriter who can only get commissioned to write black stories. She liked my autobiographical piece on cultural appropriation last time, maybe she'll like this?

Hannah isn't impressed.

'Think about the audience. Think about what's *useful* you can say to them.'

You being a screenwriter who hasn't been to university in ten years, my brain adds.

'Ok, ok.' I scramble for a new idea. 'Genre', I blurt, 'Writing. Most academics are bad at it. Horrible stylists anyway.' I'm making this up as I go along.

Positive noises down the phone.

'But really, *everything is genre,* even our identities as writers. And we should embrace that. Genre gives us structure to be creative within.'

Hannah can't be buying this?

'Cool. Do that. Deadline's end of July.'

Sweet. That's ages away, I think. I've got loads of time.

***

One week to August. A phone call.

'You still good to send me that first draft next week?'

'Of course.'

Oh shit.

I decided to begin with an account of me pitching this essay not to be flippant, but to show how similar the worlds of academic and TV writing can be. In both mediums, the same brutal facts hold sway. We write stuff we hope will find an audience. By building an audience we build our reputations and, either directly through writers' fees or indirectly through tenure and promotions, get paid. This way we continue writing.

In my original blog post, I wrote about how growing up meant learning to deal with what others expected of me, and I expected of myself, as someone with the identity of 'black man'. While I had no desire to be a stereotype, that is, *exactly* what others expect, I had to find a way to be that engaged with this identity that I couldn't help possessing, but had grown up with little experience of. In this commentary, I want to draw parallels between the acts of creating identity and creating writing. Both are exercises in expectation management, balancing conforming to others' expectations sufficiently to remain intelligible with the need to subvert them to surprise and be original.

Fiction or non-fiction, we are all storytellers. The moment-by-moment sights and sounds of ethnographic fieldwork have no more significance in isolation than the 40,000 odd words from which a fiction writer creates their story. Without shaping them into a narrative, they are meaningless. It is no coincidence that when arguments and dramatic narratives are effective, we call them both compelling. Both, correctly structured, have a beginning, a middle, and an end. A three-act structure. Each act breaking down fractally into its own beginning, middle, and end. This structure speaks to something profound about how we, as humans, have learned to engage with new information. We don't just want the facts, we want the facts to tell us a story.

It's always really pissed me off that there is a strain of thought which says, when it comes to academic writing, that telling a good story, with good writing craft, doesn't matter.

Words matter. Writing style matters. How is it that most social sciences and humanities courses offer almost no training in *writing* well? Or if they do it's something shameful, kept for the greenest or most 'behind' students and taught by the lowliest academic staff. It is a training that enforces a certain house style of what constitutes good writing, but it is a style hardly anyone in either literary circles or the general public would recognise as either clear or compelling. The argument for this 'style' goes that it is the ideas that matter, the rational 'facts' that are being told, not *how* they are communicated. This argument is clearly bollocks. Where are these ideas? They are pixels on a screen. Ink on a page. They are literally and physically the words through which they are expressed. Until somebody can take me to their Platonic Cave,[1] and show me their ideas without the unnecessary flummery of written or spoken language, I'm not changing my mind. It says something about them as thinkers that reading Wacquant feels like swimming through soup, but reading Graeber is like having a coffee with a very smart old friend (see Wacquant, 2006 and Graeber, 2004).

Back to my pitching call with Hannah. As we begin, I don't have any brilliant ideas. This is normal. Brilliant ideas are rare. In the absence of inspiration, my first idea is to go with something I think she'll like, based on my previous experience of writing for *Disruptive Inequalities*. I pitch a genre piece. A 'How my *x* Identity Constrains my *y* Story'. Here, x being 'Black' and y being 'creative practice'. Above the logline might stand '*autobiographical diversity essay 1x1500 words*'. You'll have read articles in this vein before. Like I said, it's a genre, a recognisable style with as expected and familiar a structure and set of tropes as psychological thrillers or police procedurals in TV. It's a topic I'm interested in, but it's also trendy. People like stuff about

---

[1] In The Allegory of the Cave, Plato introduces the idea that our experience of reality is akin to a person brought up in a cave, only seeing the shadows of 'real' objects cast by a flame, and taking these shadows for the object itself. Beyond our perception, he believed there existed 'ideal' objects, like the objects casting shadows in the cave, which we are only able to perceive at a remove.

identity and diversity right now. My first instinct is to leverage the genre of author I am to write a genre of story I know is popular.

I am a genre by the way. Kinda-Edgy Young-ish Black Writer. I didn't set out to be a genre, but I don't mind that I am. In fact, I play up to it. In my publicity photos I wear all black. Dungarees, boots, shirt. My head is shaved. Artsy, but a little macho. Maybe a touch reminiscent of the Black Panthers' uniform, but not so much as to be obviously wanky.

The first thing I wrote was a Yorkshire Gothic. I'm from Leeds. I knew the people I was writing. Got nowhere. When a mediocre script I wrote about teen drug dealers in Tottenham placed highly in a national competition, I got a sense of what genres commissioners were interested in *from me*. Earlier this year I was paid to write two episodes of a show about more teenage drug dealers, this time doing grime. Hadn't listened to grime since Boy In Da Corner (Rascal, 2003). I loved it. When everyone thinks they know exactly how a story is going to go, it is easy to surprise them, to give them something familiar enough, but new.

But Hannah wasn't interested in my first, somewhat lazy, idea. She wasn't interested for the most TV commissioner of reasons. I wasn't thinking about the audience. I'm not exotic to this audience because I'm black. I'm exotic because I'm a screenwriter. Write something based on that. Suddenly I know my genre.

Cue drum roll.

I will cast myself as a Campbell-esque hero with a thousand faces,[2] bringing back the boon of knowledge from my time in the barbaric lands of TV to the civilised meadows of academe. Or, to describe the genre another way, I'll do ethnography. This trope of experiencing people and places unfamiliar to the reader, be they on the other side of the world or the estate up the road, and bringing back hard-won knowledge from one's time there, is the basis of ethnographic writing. Unlike mythological heroes who use this knowledge to rescue princesses and the like, ethnographers tend to use their knowledge to either critique or bolster currently popular theoretical frameworks.

Now I know my genre I am much happier. Now I just need to make the familiar beats feel unexpected.

---

[2] Anthropologist and folklorist Joseph Campbell became famous in literary circles for his interesting but academically dubious comparative study of mythology *The Hero with a Thousand Faces* (1949), which described an archetypal 'hero's journey' that Campbell argued underpinned almost all myths. Campbell's hero's journey would go on to be the basis of the plot of the original *Star Wars*.

2.2.1 Subverting Genre Expectations

As you've probably realised, I like genre conventions. These are the rules that make a genre what it is. The mismatched lovers might have fallen out now, but it's a rom-com so I know they'll get back together in the end. I watch a lot of horror. Knowing the jump scare is coming and anticipating it is as much fun as the scare itself. I brace. My girlfriend braces for my inevitable jump and yell. Everybody enjoys themselves. When I write, I make a point of knowing the conventions of the genre I'm writing. Like the structure of a sonnet for a poet, genre constraints give a useful structure to be creative within. One of my favourite things as a writer and reader is seeing familiar genre tropes realised in an unfamiliar way. *Get Out* starts out as a seemingly grounded horror. You know Chris's white girlfriend's family are up to no good. You don't expect them to be interracial bodysnatchers. Familiar genres can also serve as a Trojan horse to smuggle subversive messages into spaces where they might otherwise not be heard. You might consider *The Purge* movies trashy, but across five films and counting they've screamed 'eat the rich, they're murdering parasites' to audiences of millions. If the form of the message is familiar, audiences can be surprisingly receptive to radical content.

Subverting genre is a balancing act. The risk is that readers might mistake what you are trying to achieve completely. Think you're writing one genre when you're really writing another. The result can be incomprehension, or even anger. This risk became particularly clear to me when I sent my most recent play, *Terror Management Theory*, to theatres. The play revolves around a dinner party which spins dangerously off the rails. Of the white readers that responded, the play was uniformly critiqued as sophomore. I was sent example scripts of more 'sophisticated' plays, all Black-with-a-capital-B theatre that, in my view, objectified black suffering for white liberal audiences. If I'd been sent *God of Carnage*, or *Who's Afraid of Virginia Woolf?* I would have understood. These are similar plays to mine, the veil of polite society being torn away across one nerve-wracking evening. My characters were wealthy film producers: why was I being sent plays about slaves and the ghetto? The answer, I expect, is 'dinner party gone to hell' is not a genre that was expected from a thirty-year-old black guy. As it was, the UK's leading black theatre company, Talawa, had it open their residency at the Fairfield Halls after eighteen months of lockdown to a uniformly enthusiastic reception. The screened performance got me a conversation with an agent. The characters were black. The genre wasn't. Only one company understood.

In academic writing, Hannah Cowan (2021) has been viciously attacked by health campaigners for her critical articles about the NHS. For them, there are only two genres. 'The NHS must be protected' and 'The NHS is bad and should be privatised'. In this binary world, there is no room for Hannah's writing in the genre of 'We can imagine a better future than what we currently have'.

***

So what am I saying? What's the takeaway? Most of all, I'm saying think about the genre you're writing in. Know it. Study it. Are you just reproducing the expected tropes, or are you subverting them to create something new that only you could make? And what is *your* genre as a writer? Are you happy with that? If not, what can you do to change it?

Academic or not, writing is your craft, and you should master it. Clear writing *is* clear thinking. Some rules of thumb, borrowed from George Orwell, are to use normal words and punctuation unless strictly necessary. Go back and look. In this commentary I've only used full stops, commas, and question marks. There is also a clear three-act structure, with each act delineated by a title or subheading. As always, writing this I felt pressure not to commit the ultimate sin of being boring. You should feel this pressure too. Strive for your writing to be enjoyable as well as informative. We're all storytellers. Whatever you're trying to communicate, make your story a good one.

3 Writing through Mess by Natassia Brenman

3.1 Blog Post

POSTED 26 JULY 2017

At the Edge-Lands of Mental Health Care, Whose Vulnerability Counts?

Figure 3.1 Edge-lands

I don't *think* I ever met the two homeless people who had been sleeping outside the counselling service I spent time volunteering at last year. I'd been there as part of a piece of research with mental health charities in London, which (with the mainstream system currently bursting at the seams) have become more important than ever as places for people to come to in their darkest hour.[3] But these two had come hoping to make use of the sheltered doorway of the centre, rather than the listening ear of a volunteer counsellor, and fairly quickly it was decided that this went beyond what the service had to offer.

And so by the time I arrived there, all that was left of the homeless pair were a jumble of vague stories, a few traces of their existence: there was the mention from the receptionist that one of the pair had popped up in the Tesco's car park a few streets away, astonished that she'd recognised him ('I think he thought he was invisible!'); sometimes people talked about the *'night revellers'* that used to leave glass bottles whose broken shards would shine in the gutters; and then there were murmurs that the mess between the breeze-blocks at the bend in the road was in fact human excrement, which apparently they used to have to get rid of with buckets of bleachy water, sluiced through the half-cobbled, half tar-macked terrain of the cul-de-sac.

Like so much of inner-city London, the neighbourhood is being bought up and developed at a rate so fast it can't keep up with itself. Despite the soaring property prices and quick turnover of shop fronts, there remain large enclaves of deprivation and buildings that haven't been touched for years. The 1960s block behind the service sits unused, as does the old gasholder behind the wire fencing. The cul-de-sac in which the service is based is privately owned, and so the responsibility to maintain it lies with the landlord and local residents. This probably explains the unfinished tarmac job, the abandoned cars that lined the opposite side of the street, and the sign, imploringly hand painted directly onto the red-brick house at the end: 'No dumping!'

When the charity's chair of trustees came in for a meeting one day a year or so ago and saw the two figures with their sleeping bags and cans scattered around them, she would have known that – without someone personally intervening – it was likely they'd still be there when next month's meeting came around. And the next. It was unclear from the titbits of story I gathered from the longer-standing members of staff whether the fears about the homeless duo's aggres-sion ever actually played out (mostly people described them in general, slightly euphemistic terms such as being 'unlovable' and 'making a mess'), but the trustees all agreed that they needed to go.

---

[3] https://theconversation.com/mental-health-is-in-no-fit-state-whatever-the-politicians-say-15743

Julie, one of the administrators, was enlisted to call the police, in the hope that they would resolve the situation. She told me about this looking out sideways from behind her computer monitor, an elbow on the desk, looking defiant. She hadn't wanted to call the police; her conviction was *'either you help someone with your whole heart, or you just leave them be'*. But they kept asking, and she didn't think they would have appreciated her opinion. So she kept calling, until they were gone.

Months later, I was asked to come to one of the trustee meetings to present some of my research findings about their service users' experiences of accessing counselling. I had been interested in what it had felt like for new clients encountering the service for the first time. One of the people I spoke to – I called her Claire – had never accessed a mental health service before. She had been waiting to see a bereavement counsellor on the NHS for almost two years, which had left her feeling mistrustful of promises of free care and support. Approaching the charity for her initial assessment, her heart had sunk when she saw the rusty sign and deserted cul-de-sac. She'd had a strong sense that there could be a man in the bushes, waiting to jump out at her, and there wouldn't be anyone around to help.

As I recounted this to the board of trustees and management of the charity, amongst tea and biscuits and home-made rock-cakes, they listened intently, their faces tired and concerned. When I finished talking, it was the imaginary man in the bushes that seemed to have captured everyone's attention. One of the board members informed me that this wasn't so far from the truth, that there *had* in fact, last year, been two men hanging around outside the service. I of course knew exactly whom she was talking about. Without going into exactly how they had managed to get them to 'move on', the chair explained that they were no longer there to upset vulnerable clients coming to the service. She made eye contact with me as she said the word 'vulnerable', signalling to me that Claire's story had been taken seriously, that her vulnerability was something that they were accountable for.

It made me feel deeply uncomfortable that (read backwards at least) my research findings seemed to be justifying the forced removal of the two home-less people, and suggesting that further 'cleansing' of the area was necessary to protect clients like those who had participated in my study. Perhaps more uncomfortable was the truth that Claire *was* vulnerable and that the threat (real or imagined) of encountering strangers in this space was heightening the fears and anxieties that had brought her to the service in the first place.

But my discomfort wasn't just about unwelcome truths. It was about the fact that the story I heard was precluding some important questions being asked. The first was about what was being made invisible through the actual removal of the two men, and the subsequent haze and ambiguity in which the story was shrouded. The threat that they actually posed was obscured by the euphemistic ways of talking about how they were putting clients off, and by the conflicting stories about how and why they were removed in the end. Oddly, amongst all of the perceived threats in this story, only one came to fruition: the threat from the trustees to forcibly reclaim the space that had at some point seemed a safe place to inhabit. Also made invisible was the men's vulnerability. Despite the references to *street drinkers* or *night revellers*, the traces of makeshift bed and toilet suggest that this had been a site of a very precarious existence, which had of course in the end been criminalised and dismantled. Ultimately, this process of invisiblisation seemed to answer the question (before it had been asked) of whose vulnerability *counts*.

Mental health problems and homelessness are without doubt closely intertwined issues in inner city contexts like this,[4] particularly as services in both areas continue to be cut across sectors. The small charity I have been talking about hasn't chosen to take on this particular intersection of disadvantage, and nor is it their responsibility to so. They have decided to focus on the needs of a different client group, who are *also* vulnerable and have needs that often aren't met by mainstream services. But maybe a useful question to ask is whether this decision really has to be a trade-off, whereby helping some necessitates the removal of others? This could help us hold in sight multiple vulnerabilities, some of which we can address, and some of which we could simply, as Julie says, 'leave be'.

3.2 Commentary

This blog post was one of the first pieces I wrote from my doctoral research: an 'ethnography of access' in mental health care, based within a small cluster of voluntary sector psychotherapy services in inner-city London. These services work to include people who are absent or excluded from both public and privately paid-for mental health care settings; groups who are often referred to in public health as the 'hard-to-reach'. I eventually wrote my PhD in two parts, about 'place' and 'need', exploring how both produced inclusions and exclusions in interconnected ways. Having started off as an exercise in working through and letting off steam about an uncomfortable set of encounters in the field, this short blog post ended up helping me to develop my methodological approach to 'placing' the issues I was writing about. This involved a creative interview method, in which I asked people to visually map places and their first

---

[4] www.mungos.org/publication/final-report-st-mungos-call-4-evidence-mental-health-street-homelessness/

encounters with them, as well as a style of ethnographic writing in which I described people, identities, and relationships 'in place' (Brenman, 2019). This approach helped to make visible the hard work it took to create and maintain inclusive places for people who may not 'belong' elsewhere in the mental health system. Ironically, carrying out this work under conditions of austerity ended up positioning service users and providers in the voluntary sector *always almost* on the outside of this very system of care.

In this commentary, I take myself back to one particular place and reflect on the methods and potential effects of writing the spatial arrangements and socio-material mess of this 'edge-land of mental health care'. First, how I materialised the messy politics of in/exclusion, inviting the reader to become immersed in them with me; and second, how situating a particular problem can help both writer and reader hold moral and ethical tensions 'in place'. I build on methodologies that describe the 'mess' of the social world (Law, 2004), and have been inspired by those that are 'inventive', meaning they are part of creating worlds rather than just describing them. In other words, methodologies 'oriented towards making a difference' (Wakeford & Lury, 2012, p. 11). In this case, I used research practices that produced many different versions of the same place, which in turn produced many possible ways to intervene in the politics of place-making. I want to take the opportunity to raise questions about what work this kind of ethnographic writing can do, and perhaps undo, when it comes to materialising vulnerabilities and inequalities.

3.2.1 Materialising Messy Politics

In asking 'whose vulnerability counts?', I was grappling with what story to tell – the mundane account of 'tidying up' the threshold of the counselling service to make it more welcoming to distressed clients, or the more uncomfortable one, which acknowledged that this 'tidying up' involved the removal of the two homeless people. This second story was already heavily anecdotalised (Micheal, 2012) by the staff at the clinic, with my retelling of it making the whole situation increasingly *un*tidy. Moreover, such an anecdote could never represent the normal happenings of my field sites. However, I used this *particular* happening to tell a story of matter out of place (Douglas, 1966) *and* people out of place (Ahmed, 2000), in order to say something important about how in/exclusion is enacted in a particular landscape of care. The anecdote could be described in the words of Lauren Berlant (referencing Susan Leigh Star's ethnographies of infrastructure) as a 'glitch of the present': a unique happening that serves as 'a revelation of what had been the lived ordinary' (Berlant, 2015,

p. 403). In other words, the removal of the two homeless people occurred in isolation from all the ordinary dilemmas of access and belonging, but nevertheless can be seen within a wider assemblage of comings and goings to give a different perspective on how therapeutic places are made and remade, and for whom. Reading the piece back, I see that the moral and ethical dilemma was not just about making claims about 'whose vulnerability counts?' but how to tell the story of this question as it emerged and was being answered at different moments and from different positions in a particular place. Writing the messy telling and retelling of the anecdote was a good starting point: conjuring up multiple voices telling competing stories 'in place' highlighted the crucial absence of two homeless protagonists' voices, who were by then long gone from the scene.

It was of course 'the scene' itself that ended up doing much of the storytelling. But this involves important choices and techniques of writing and observing: Donna Haraway (2016, p. 12) articulates this need to attend to the materials (environments, actors, objects) we use to create stories and possible worlds, writing, 'it matters which stories make worlds, what worlds make stories'. The world I was studying was one located at the doors of mental health services, with issues of access and eligibility most obviously playing out in waiting rooms, front desks, clinical assessment meetings, and so on. But when I found myself a few metres away from the front door of the clinic, standing over the famous breeze-block corner and staring down at the traces of (potentially human) 'mess', I was nudging up against another world: one that made a more complicated story than the one on the other side of the door to the counselling service. As ethnographers, we can sensitise ourselves to these traces of messier worlds, and in our writing of them begin to materialise different stories about the 'often invisible side of inequality' that this Element is all about (Del Percio and Cowan, Section 1).

Immersing the reader in details of bits of broken glass, recently cleaned-up excrement, a half-tarmacked private road, and the imploring sign of 'no dumping!' documented the tidying up of mess, but also of people. This came from a decision to notice people and materials beyond the obvious boundaries of the field site and led to an analysis about 'dumping' and 'tidying' in systems of care that might not otherwise have emerged. The everyday work of 'tidying up' that staff engaged in reflected the marginalised position of the organisation in the broader landscape of care. This, in turn, resulted in a politics of inclusion and exclusion that raised the questions I explore in the piece about 'whose vulnerability counts?' In this way, writing becomes a materialising practice: one that can surface questions worth asking, even when they complicate the story that you thought you were going to tell.

3.2.2 Holding Moral Tensions 'In Place'

This materialising practice of leading with place (letting the scene tell the story) can also cause problems: messy writing makes for messy moral work. In my ethnography, I used mapping techniques with service users to invoke socio-material accounts of their first encounters with mental health care settings. This generated visual data that helped demonstrate how precarity is created in place (Brenman, 2020). In the blog piece, I describe the embodied sense of vulnerability and unfamiliarity of the woman I call Claire when she accessed the service by recounting her concern with the rusty sign and deserted cul-de-sac; material and spatial details that coloured her experience of finally being offered her course of counselling sessions after a two-year wait for therapy with the National Health Service. But I also document my discomfort at how this account took on a life of its own when I shared it with the clinical staff I'd been working with. Her lively depiction of an imagined 'man in the bushes' did not just prompt concern for a new client; it also justified the forced removal of the two homeless men. As a result, Claire's vulnerability was pitted against that of the homeless people – with hers clearly winning out.

By letting these multiple stories emerge and coexist in the same place, new interpretations and possible exclusions were able to form in ways I wasn't comfortable with. And so 'placing' can do the evocative work of making certain things visible but it can also *un*do the ethnographer's careful moral and ethical framing of a situation. The situated framing I chose (like a still camera with people coming in and out of a scene) is a different methodological choice to following the journeys and perspectives of certain people. It points to the limits as well as the possibilities of leading with place rather than people, but it is also what politicises this materialising and messy writing practice. While writers never have complete control over their text, I propose that 'placing' issues in this way brings further riskiness to ethnographic writing, which can offer up more power to the reader. This includes the power to participate in the observations and make their own judgements about complex situations and the questions that arise from them ('whose vulnerability counts?' being just one of many questions the reader might want to ask for themselves). My use of the idea of riskiness echoes Fitzgerald and Callard's (2016) 'ambiguous and risky intellectual space', but is about becoming entangled in material rather than disciplinary spaces: the risks that we (as observers and writers) run when we find ourselves entangled in situations where we might lose control of a story and its morals.

I have been arguing that 'placing' problems and writing through their mess is a productive means to materialise banal inequalities. This involves bringing these less visible inequalities to the surface through risky, potentially uncomfortable, writing practices. In describing 'actual' or material mess, we can bring forth messier worlds that complicate more obvious forms of inequalities that are described in different kinds of writing. In my work, I sought to disrupt the politically neutral narratives of 'barriers and facilitators' that frame problems of access to care in public health by situating these problems in very specific social and material arrangements. One way to repoliticise these problems in ethnographic writing is to tell stories as they emerge from particular (often peripheral, and therefore less visible) places, attending to the multiple accounts and the traces of absent others that come into view. This kind of writing can arrange stories in space and time so that ethical and moral tensions within them are not resolved or 'tidied up', but rather held 'in place'.

4 On Poverty Porn by Alfonso Del Percio

4.1 Blog Post

POSTED 2 JUNE 2020
**Freedom, Oppression, Sacrifice: Chronicles from the Italian Lockdown
(Part Two)**

Figure 4.1 Freeeee! Author's image.

I want to buy a car. I want my freedom back. Freeeee! The government has
announced a softening of the lockdown. People can move now within their
region. The radio clarifies that social distancing still needs to be maintained, it
has become part of our 'new normality'. Wear masks, keep distance, don't hug,
stand in line, don't gather. But moving, moving is allowed. I need a car. I want to
bring the kids to the mountains. Cambiamento d'aria (change of air), people call
it here. I saw an advert from Andrei, a Romanian man living in the neighbouring
town who wants to sell his Renault. It is cheap, an old car, but still a strong
engine, he tells me on the phone. But migrants spread the virus, people kept
telling me. Are you sure you want to buy a car from a gipsy? They carry the
virus.

Migrants are super-spreaders, agrees Legame, a social cooperative with
which I have been collaborating since 2015. It provides services to workers
which are employed by the Southern Italian agricultural industries.

Romanians, Bulgarians, Ukrainians, but also Moroccans and many workers from sub-Saharan Africa. It has been operating not far from here in a little town famous for its tomato plantations. Migrants are virus spreaders, they are convinced. This is why, last month, they decided to translate the rules of social distancing, including hygiene guidelines, into as many languages as possible. So that migrants too would eventually be able to understand what to do to avoid the spreading of the virus. This concern for migrants' infectability is part of a larger campaign aimed at empowering migrants. Along with what sociolinguists have been preaching for decades, their practice assumes that translating information from the state can help fight structures of inequality. If only people can use their first language this world would be a better one.

We know from historians that this assumption is not new. The violent colonisation of the world through imperial power has always co-existed with the spread of civilising and modernising knowledge. Translation as a technique of persuasion allowed colonisers to localise knowledge, to adapt it to the world views and modes of living of the individuals targeted and to create consent for the occupation and dispossession of territories as well as violence and oppression. Translating hygiene and public health measures was a means of imposing knowledge about the human body that, while seemingly benevolent, positioned the colonised as subordinate and produced a racialised critique of people's cultural practices and social relations.

I can give you a discount, clarifies Andrei. He sounds desperate. Buying a car from a Romanian? No no, not now, people insist. I meet him in his neighbourhood. Massimo, a friend of mine, gave me a lift by car. Buses have stopped running. It is my first time here. Deserts of concrete. Big, overcrowded houses. Families squeezed in small apartments. Children playing on tiny balconies. Others meeting on the building's stairs. I think about the houses in the neighbouring town in which we live. Terraced houses. Gardens with a sea view. Eighty percent of the buildings are empty, waiting for tourists to come. Wealth and poverty exist side by side in this part of Italy. What if migrants' major infectability is caused not by language, not by migrants' lack of understanding of the confinement rules, but by these housing inequalities? What if it is not the virus that makes people die, but the system of inequality that we have built around us?

I see Andrei come down the stairs. He limps. He tells me later that he had almost lost his leg in a work accident in a firework factory. People here are crazy about fireworks. I instinctively tried to shake his hand. My body forgot that body contact needs to be absolutely avoided. Greetings are out in times of Covid-19. Andrei looks at me astonished. He knows the rules. No need for translation.

Figure 4.2 Lockdown homes. Author's image.

Are you crazy, his eyes seem to say, keep your distance. I apologise. Try to say something about routines. And about how they come automatically to justify my misbehaviour. But he does not seem to listen. This is the car. It is an old vehicle. I used to drive to Romania with it. Three thousand kilometres. Three times already. The coachwork is damaged. Dents here, scratches there. But I have not used it for ages, I don't need it anymore.

I knew he was lying. Before leaving me alone with Andrei, Massimo insisted we check him. His habits. His car. You never know, explained Massimo. This is Italy. You can't trust people. Be careful, he insisted. We should ask around

Figure 4.3 New car. Author's image.

before buying, he advised. We had stopped at a Romanian bakery in the block. Bought some bread. Chatted with people. The women behind the counter knew Andrei. She wore a mask. She knew the rules. No need for translations. He has three kids. Hard worker. He drinks, but we all do, added a man who was smoking a cigarette in front of the bakery. He does not make any trouble. He uses his car to drive his family. To go to work. But he does not transport any material. No concrete, no tools. The car is fine. You can take it. Massimo agreed. He is going to give you a good price. He needs the money.

Andrei makes a good deal. I don't negotiate. I need the car. Freedom. His children observe the scene from their balcony. Silent.

We sit in the car and drive to Eugenio's office to process the transfer of ownership of the vehicle. The transfer of ownership needs to be visible to the state. And the state wants you to pay taxes for this transaction. They want a slice of the cake, laughs Eugenio while explaining the procedure to me. Eugenio and Andrei seem to know each other. How is work going, Eugenio asks. Work? I thought that the country was in lockdown. Stay home they said. I assumed that construction work had stopped, factories closed. I get to know that the lockdown was not for everybody. It isn't just doctors, nurses and other care workers working. Andrei was working too. Hidden from the vigilance of the authorities. But working. While signing forms and waiting for the printer to work, I found out that Andrei had been working as a day labourer. Sometimes painting the wooden windows of buildings that had been damaged by the sun. Sometimes on a construction site. Sometimes in the fields picking fruits and vegetables. Sometimes doing other small stuff. Somebody needs to keep labouring, Eugenio notes. We can't all stay home.

I had heard about the government's need for manpower in the fields to keep the provision of food going. Along with what was happening in other countries in Europe they wanted to organise charter flights to fly in workers from eastern Europe; to do the work that Italians don't want to do. There was also the idea to legalise informal agricultural labourers. The army of illegalised, black bodies that, yesterday, large sectors of the Italian public wanted to send back 'home', perhaps then to be drowned in the Mediterranean Sea, now had to save the nation. The economy needs to restart, politicians kept repeating. But this was different. There was a parallel economy of labour which continued operating despite the lockdown. Invisible. With no security measures. No distancing. No protection. Are migrants super-spreaders? Or are they deliberately exposed to the risk of infection? Is language then perhaps just an excuse to avoid speaking about their exposure? Their exploitation? Their sacrifice?

Where is your mask? Eugenio laughs. Leave the office, he shouts with a smile. Can't you read the signs at the door? Don't you understand our language? How long have you been here Andrei? Twenty years? Can't you read? This is a public office. You need a mask. Don't you understand the significance of confinement? C-O-N-F-I-N-E-M-E-N-T. The language question again. Eugenio was joking of course. He had been enfacing his questions with an exaggerated sarcastic smile. As if he wanted to make fun of this assumption that people would not understand the rules. Or was he serious? Andrei had warned me about Eugenio's humour: You never know what he means. I think he is crazy.

Screw the masks. Screw the virus, Andrei brings me back into the office. Eugenio is still trying to make the printer work. His office looks like a mix between a public office and the smoky place where my father used to play cards in Switzerland when I was a child. Piles of documents. And old computers. Posters of naked women on the walls. Bunting from Italy's major football teams. Printers. A lot of printers. Screw the virus, he repeats. The virus is a business, Andrei adds. They want me to pay for your virus. Eugenio nodded, while reinitiating the printer. It is a business, Andrei shouts. Fuck them. Employers call us one day, and the other day they don't. One day they pay. One day they don't. Fuck them. Fuck them. They treat us like animals. Animals. Fuck them. Eugenio laughs. He can't stop laughing. Is he really crazy?

How will you go to work now? Eugenio laughs at Andrei while asking me to sign a document. How will you go to work now? Andrei, we need you to work.

Work. Somebody needs to work. We need to keep going. You have no car. How will you go to work? Eugenio laughs again. Andrei needed the car. The woman in the bakery was right. He needs the car. For work. To drive his children to school. To go to Romania. He can't afford to buy flight tickets. Buses are expensive too. He needs the car.

After having signed all papers, I drive Andrei home. Drive, it is yours. He asks me to stop him next to a letting agency. I will walk, he notes. I insist on driving him home. I will walk. He opens the car door and leaves with the envelope of money in his hand. He had held the envelope during the entire process. I start to think that he needed the money to pay his rent. I can't get rid of this idea. Does he need the money to pay his rent? Did he enter the letting agency? I don't dare to watch in the rear-view mirror. Or is he meeting a usurer? I had read in the media that people were struggling to pay their rents. That people had started to borrow money from loan sharks to cover the loss of salaries. That people working informally had not benefited from the financial support provided by the government to those who had become unemployed because of the lockdown. The mafia has supplanted the state, a national news-paper headline stated. I was hearing about these businesses profiting from those who were struggling. Was he making enough money? Was he selling his car to compensate the loss of salary and pay his rent?

I drive home with a feeling of freedom and, at the same time, a sensation of despair. Joy and sadness, freedom and submission, wealth and poverty, hope and despair have never seemed so close to me. Next to an Italian flag I see a big poster at a balcony decorated with the colours of the rainbow. We will all get through this if we stay home and hold together, it says. What if instead of holding together, instead of practising solidarity, what will make us get through this is the suffering of others? This is not good, I think. My freedom, my ability to see the mountains seems to happen at the cost of others. I realise that inequality is not, or not only about unequal consumption, but about consumption enabled by oppression. In this moment, driving home from this transaction, I realise that I am the oppressor. I am part of a privileged section of our society that oppresses. I have no doubts our collective ability to overcome this health crises and its social and economic effects will depend on the necessity of others to sacrifice themselves. More than solidarity then what seems to me the motif of this crises is submission, servitude, and oppression. The sacrifice of others' lives. Language is here to make us forget this: We are all in this together. The question of language and translation is here to help us avoid having to speak about sacrifice, about the violence that people like me exert on others. Language makes us avoid taking responsibility for the costs of our enjoyment.

Banal oppression. Banal inequality occurs trough banal oppression. While shutting the door of the car, I think that it is through these seemingly mundane practices, such as buying an old car, hiding oneself behind the presumed empowering nature of language and translation, that both oppression and inequality manifests itself. We are used to putting the blame on others, on the big corporations, on the capitalist conspiracy, on the state, on god, and tend to forget that inequality's most powerful weapon is the banality of everyday practices, choices and decisions. Our seemingly mundane actions are what makes inequality and oppression stick. What makes it bearable and acceptable. What makes it normal. Within any moment, we can all be the oppressor. Here, I am the oppressor. Oppression is what makes me free.

4.2 Commentary

How do we write about inequality, poverty, oppression, and exploitation without running the risk that our stories feed into systems of violence and exploitation? Without them becoming poverty porn, emotion, even entertainment or enjoyment for the powerful at the expense of the poor? Poverty porn is when we collect and write stories of poverty, pain, oppression, and humiliation for commodification or for the sake of entertaining privileged audiences. These accounts of suffering often reproduce the script of fairy tales, feel-good stories of compassion, but also of saving heroes (often Western, white, rich men) that require the continued existence of poverty to maintain their status as saviours of the oppressed. Therefore, poverty porn does not only reassure. It provides a distorted picture of inequality and contributes to the normalisation of the harms it accounts for. Think of those charity campaigns using hard-hitting images such as pictures of malnourished children with flies in their eyes, protruding ribcage, runny nose, and extended hands toward the camera that help powerful, rich donors feel needed, even essential to the transformation of the structures of inequality that they in fact produce.

When writing banal inequality in our blog *Disruptive Inequalities*, I feel that the danger of producing poverty porn is imminent. While poverty porn can be found in every writing about people and social inequality, I also think that the thick ethnographic writing, the meticulous portrayal of human suffering that we privilege in our blog, exposes us to a danger of fetishising stories of humiliation, oppression. This risk was evident for me when, in 2020, I started to write *Freedom, Oppression, Sacrifice: Chronicles from the Italian Lockdown*. I wanted to document the lockdown measures in Southern Italy where we had moved to with my family to spend my sabbatical. I wanted to portray the conditions of the migrant population and document how the pandemic had exacerbated the relations of inequality in one of the poorest regions in Southern Europe. I intended to choose a language that allowed me to get close to these complex dynamics of inequality and the feelings of despair that inform them. It took me several weeks to write that short piece. I kept putting the text aside, starting again, changing the frame, adapting the characters, fabricating a new plot. I struggled with the idea that my piece would reproduce the same old, reassuring fairy tale script that I intend to contest. There had to be another way of characterising their conditions.

Rather than becoming the interpreter of oppressed others saved by a member of the very system producing their oppression, I wanted to redirect my writing to the circumstances that produce pain, oppression, and inequality. The oppressed subjects had to remain in the background of my account. While it can be politically relevant to amplify people's attempts to make life worth living, their alliances, and collective attempts to struggle against oppressive systems, the danger of appropriating these stories, to fetishise and romanticise them, to distort them for one's own sake, to use them to make myself look like a hero was something I wanted to avoid. I rather wanted to depict in detail the complex logics, that is, the histories, the places, the people, their feelings, and assumptions that produce inequality and subalternity. Rather than constructing a story that centres oppressed people and their voices, my account had to focus on the banality of inequality, the social forces, the dynamics of power, including the temporal and spatial formations that shape people, their stories, and the unequal positions they occupy in society.

To avoid reproducing problematic, old-known saved vs. saviour narratives, my account had to open up new meanings, multiple connections, dissonant scripts. It had to link stories about migration and poverty to accounts of public health, colonialism, and racial stigma, but also housing disparities, work exploitation, madness, and translation. I had to construct around my story a complex set of relations, to introduce multiple temporalities, to write about Southern Italy in 2020, but also to tell stories about colonial history, and to write the present and the past as closely intertwined. I tried to interconnect feelings, spaces, and practices that we usually imagine as separate: buying a car, labour in fireworks factories, translation in NGOs, spying on somebody in a Romanian bakery, limping down the stairs of an overcrowded house, watching posters of naked women in a public office, children playing on a balcony, fruit picking, but also histories of health, translation, and racial stigma. I also wanted to present the multiple rationales underpinning confinement and the regulation of the migrant population during the pandemic – empowerment, care, control, discipline, freedom, exploitation. All this to decentre the perverse narratives of pain and suffering that we are all addicted to and like to consume, and rather foreground the relations of privilege and exploitation that constitute them.

I am not intending that people's stories should not be told and heard. That we should silence the stories of the oppressed. I rather intend that these are not our stories; we don't own them. Our stories are different. They are written from another positionality, from that of an observing witness. We cannot speak for the oppressed, but we can tell our own stories in a way that enables us to engage in a shared struggle for change, to create alliances with other people longing for transformation, including those who experience oppression and exclusion. What we can bring to these alliances is our training in social analysis, the capacity we have acquired to use writing, narrativisation, and storytelling to document, understand, and foreground the multiple and sometimes even confusing and contradictory layers banal inequality consists of.

I found that one powerful way to document these layers constituting banal inequality is to put a material object at the centre of my account, for example a car, around which then multiple interconnected stories could be told. Stories of freedom, of mobility and privilege. Stories of suspicion, racial stigma, and super-spreaders. Stories of labour and work exploitation. Stories of bureaucracy, state control, and madness. Stories of language, translation, and public health. Stories of poverty and wealth, luxury, and overdue rents as well as sacrifice, oppression, hope, and despair. Poverty porn usually works with sensational pictures, telling monolithic, unidirectional stories. Putting a car at the centre of my multiple intertwined accounts, developing a sense of the detail, depicting through close descriptions the complex nature of the material and affective dynamics that shape inequality was an attempt for me to stress the banality, mundane nature of poverty and oppression, including the multiple, and in certain cases contradictory, stories of which poverty is made.

To disrupt the fairy tale, feel-good script and the saved/saviour narrative around which this script is usually organised, it was important for me to display my own privilege as a crucial part of the stories I intended to tell. When we write, we often tend to situate privilege in one of the many 'others' we document. The privileged are always the others. While we have learned to acknowledge that as academics we hold positions of privilege, our writings often erase how this privilege operates in the encounters with the many subjects and experiences that feed the stories we write. My privileges had not just to be foregrounded. The entire storyline had to be organised around this position of privilege and power. I intended to display how my desires and egoisms contributed to the shape of my environment and social relations, how they reproduced and naturalised racial stigma, how they fed into relations of oppression and exploitation. This choice was motivated by the necessity to demonstrate that, depending on the social situations in which we end up, we can all be the oppressor. I can be the oppressor; you are the oppressor. They are the oppressor. And we oppress often without realising it, especially when holding positions of power.

Finally, to keep multiplying the meanings of the story of banal inequality I intended to tell, I wanted to put doubt at the centre of my stories. Both to depict myself as a doubting subject, to foreground my uncertainties, and to tell stories with no truths. Writing the doubts, my doubts, but also the doubts of others, writing about what triggers the doubt, never coming to fixed conclusions, never closing the range of possibilities; this is what I imagined my story to be made of. Poverty porn has no doubts, but needs to depict bolt, sensational, often over-simplified, and incomplete stories to generate sympathy for selling, donations, and support. Differently, writing banal inequalities had to be both realistic and impressionistic. Accurate, detailed, unembellished portrayals of social life, rejecting artificiality and idealisation of the social condition, yes, but also with a focus on change, movement, transition, and experience, and on less conventional and rigid modes of writing the social.

Less conventional writing is however not in itself changing the hegemonic fairy tale script that produces so much harm. The problem with the pleasurable, alternative forms of ethnographic writing that are becoming fashionable in academic writing is that, like poverty porn, they speak to the readers' desire for aestheticised accounts of poverty and inequality. This quest for aestheticisation of poverty so often comes with the necessity to meet standardised expectations of narratability and beauty, which as we know from Pierre Bourdieu are socially normalised and appeal to readers' class expectations, that is, allow readers to cultivate, display, and experience status distinction. I want my writing to be different. My stories should not reassure and gratify the powerful's classed and gendered instincts for pleasure, compassion, harmony, charity, and reconciliation. Nor should they create compliance for or legitimise a system which is fed by and capitalises on the exploitation of the harm and inequality it produces.

I want my stories to be a microscopic account of the spectacle of privilege, oppression, and inequality that surrounds us, and that produces, benefits from, and exploits inequality. The focus needs to shift away from images of malnourished children and accounts of suffering towards a petrifying scrutiny of power and expose the inner composition of the oppressive worlds we inhabit. My obsession with the details, with the mundane, the ordinary conditions of social life, my zooming into the everyday manifestations of inequality needs to make the privileged tremble, not have pleasure. I want my stories to provoke, to overwhelm, to disrupt. I want them to be polemical and antagonistic, to riot (see Sibo's text in Section 6 for an elaboration on writing as rioting). Writing needs to disturb, not gratify. It needs to reach out and seek alliances with other actors' stories, other forms of rioting, other utopias, and contribute to a transformative narrative of contemporary social life.

5 Writing the Other by Amal Latif

5.1 Blog Post

POSTED 8 DECEMBER 2020
With Love, from a Non-expendable Citizen

Figure 5.1 A street in Assam, India, 2019. Author's image.

> '*I should like to be able to love my country and still love justice. I don't want any greatness for it, particularly a greatness born of blood and falsehood. I want to keep it alive by keeping justice alive.*' Albert Camus (1961: 3–4)

I never thought much about my identity as an Indian. It felt just like breathing. I have travelled to many parts of this country, fourteen states, to be exact. From the North-Eastern part of India to the South, I have witnessed its many faces. Its streets. The perfectly round *golgappas* (an Indian street snack).

The heart-shaped red balloons. The *chai waala* (tea seller) who smiles at me every time I pass that mundane street. That woman with a basket of grapes and her recycled dreams. Also, those posters of politicians begging for votes in the name of God and nationalism. I have witnessed it all in my life as an Indian.

But ever since I enrolled for college six years ago, I have had to spend most of my time debating and proving how 'Indian' I am. Eventually, I realised that the right-wing regime and the rising communal tension in the country reduced me to my immediate identity of being a Muslim. With time, I noticed that my name mattered every time I dissented. In the middle of a casual debate at a conference, I remember a man telling me, 'Ah, I know exactly where you come from', as he heard my name. My name and my father's name decided the weight of the arguments I raised. From being harassed on social media for sharing a piece of news reporting Muslims being lynched by an invisible mob that preached 'Ahimsa' (non-violence) to being judged in academic spaces for my opinions, it all became the new normal in my everyday life. I eventually avoided revealing my identity as a Muslim when I travelled. At any social occasion, if you are asked your name and say you are Hussain, Ahmed, or Ayesha, note the reaction of the people around. Eventually, I stopped feeling the ease of being an Indian Muslim anymore. Self-confidence and hope had begun to seem blurry in my existence.

The proposal of the Citizenship Amendment Bill (CAA) in 2019 was a blood-curdling time in my life as an Indian Muslim. I remember watching the television on the edge of my seat when the Indian government passed it as an Act. My existence as an Indian was socially questioned all the while, and now it has become a legal battle. The CAA seeks to demarcate and exclude Muslims, regularising everyone's citizenship in the country except for the Muslims. For the first time in India's long history of secularism, a religious test has been enacted for granting citizenship under the passed Bill. The law specifically fast-tracks asylum claims of non-Muslim irregular immigrants from the neighbouring Muslim-majority countries of Afghanistan, Bangladesh, and Pakistan. After seventy years of freedom, to be told to prove that I am an Indian is to experience a feeling akin to shame. The Bill has led to fears among the millions of Indian Muslims. There were subsequent attacks on the minority, asking them to prove their 'Indianness'. A video from Delhi went viral in February 2020 showing five injured men lying on the street being beaten by several policemen and forced to sing the Indian national anthem. One of the men, Faizan, a twenty-three-year-old Muslim, died from his injuries two days later.

With the Bill, I witnessed family gatherings where parents advised the kids not to raise their voices, no matter what. I was told that I had no other choice if I wanted to remain safe in these mad times. I saw dire fear in the eyes of those parents as they said that. Every time I raised criticism against the brute majoritarianism, I noticed that I was losing friends with time. They raised eyebrows as I questioned the growing political polarisation in my country. Their neutrality haunted me in every political debate we had. I missed classes because I didn't feel like facing people anymore. The alienation due to the new political reality felt so real that I isolated myself from people who could not empathise with the situation. Their decision to be unapologetically apolitical at this point *is* political. That decision signifies an implicit endorsement of the current dehumanisation of citizens based on religion. I grew more and more despondent.

The animosity towards Muslim people in India of course has a long history to it, which stems from British colonial rule. While there was a lack of common unity in India beforehand, the Partition of Bengal in 1905 and the creation of separate religious electorates in 1909 by the British generated new animosity, leading to the bloody partition of a Hindu India and a Muslim Pakistan which killed almost one million people. For a time, before independence in 1947, the British conquest brought about an idea of shared suffering and community resistance within India; the test of loyalty to the nation was all about the opposition to British rule. But today, India is witnessing an upsurge in Hindu nationalist politics marked by the resumption of the long legacy of bloodshed that Indian history witnessed from British colonial rule.

India is now witnessing the chauvinistic 'patriotism' that Samuel Johnson described as the 'last refuge of the scoundrel'. Under the aegis of Hindutva fundamentalist groups, narratives of nationalism are intricately woven with narratives of religiously oriented mythology. The classic blend of emphasising national identity and Hindu religion has led to the country's divisiveness, further leading to violence. The Citizenship Act has been joined by mob lynchings of Muslims, a beef ban, and *gau rakshaks* (cow protection vigilante groups). We are suddenly in a position where eating beef has emerged as a political act of subversion in today's India. Today, to be an Indian is to submit to dogmas, rather than the demands of one's conscience. As Orwell put it, we have come to a point where 'Facts are selected or suppressed to make a case; if need be, the necessary facts are simply invented or, contrariwise, erased.'

Given the apathy of the people around me to this situation, I was relieved to see that a number of civil movements sprung up across the country with the Bill. Perhaps, this country's conscience is not that weak, I began to hope. One among them that gained global attention was the Shaheen Bagh movement. Muslim women, many clad in *burqa*s and scarves, from different backgrounds, the working, the old and young, huddled in one stretch of a highway in protest for over a hundred days. The women who were deemed as subjugated and oppressed came out to the streets to liberate their fellow citizens. Creativity is the most critical foundation of Shaheen Bagh's being. The protest proved its dynamism by singing songs of resistance to translate the art of resistance to an ordinary language. Here, we have an incredible story of how a group of Muslim women and Dadis, with their children and grandchildren, in the middle of a cold December, were choosing to peacefully resist what they believed to be unconstitutional citizenship laws targeting minorities. They chanted, '*Goli nahi phool barsao*' ('Don't rain bullets, rain flowers'). As the ordinary women spoke to the media and people, they unfolded their vocabulary of love against the systematic dehumanisation of the minority. With time, people from different communities joined the movement and something stirred in me. It was probably hope, hope that I can go back to a life where I don't have to prove my existence as an Indian Muslim.

Figure 5.2 Bilkis Bano (aged 82) holding the image of B. R. Ambedkar, recognised as the 'Father of the Constitution of India' at the Shaheen Bagh protest. Image by Vijay Pandey (2020).

The close liaison that grew between the most educated young Indian students and the Anti-CAA movement alarmed the right-wing regime. The Shaheen Bagh movement wasn't something that came out of nowhere. It resulted from years of brute majoritarianism, arrests of political leaders who dared to dissent, the brutal killings of civilians and children in Kashmir by the Indian force. It was about more than the lethal CAA. The 'integration' of Muslims was never completely achieved – even after India's independence from the British, Muslims remained the expendable 'other'. The community was also systematically used as an electoral tool by political parties. And Shaheen Bagh was an answer to all of it. It's about the women who came out to the streets to save the last ounce of secular democracy that's left in the country. And this event in the history of India will not be forgotten. The years of fear I carried on my shoulders began to feel a little lighter. I felt connected to the hundreds of women who chose to throw themselves into the streets as an act of resistance. And this connection wasn't just about my identity as an Indian Muslim woman; it was also about the oppression and fear that was inflicted upon the community for a very long time.

The Covid-19 pandemic turned out to just renew the stigma faced by the minority in the country. In March 2020, the day before the national lockdown in India, I booked a ticket and rushed to the airport to reach home as quickly as possible. My cab driver was quite impressive. He talked about how he has fixed rates for his rides, unlike the other drivers who charged as they liked. I asked him about his family. We discussed politics, education, and a lot more. After forty minutes of the drive, he opened his phone to show a forwarded video he got on WhatsApp. In the video, a white man (as far as I could make out from it) spat on a Metro train's metal pole. After he showed me the video, he said something surprising. The driver told me that the man in the video was a Muslim and he is trying to infect the others with Covid-19. I had no idea on what ground that video was shared with that description. That's what the forwarded message was, and the man bought it. He continued, '*sab musalmaan log aise hi hain, ma'am*' ('This is how all Muslims are'), filled with anger as he said that.

The lack of stereotypical markers must have made him feel that I am not a Muslim. Well, I know it because this is not the first time I have experienced bias and bigotry for the religion I belong to. This time, it felt a little different. For a very long time, I shrugged off such remarks thrown at me, as I had done since I was a young girl. It did not hit me hard – that is until my identity as an Indian was questioned. That day, I realised that I have grown up to be a different person. I did not want to run away anymore though there was so much to be afraid of. As I was about to get out of the cab, the cab driver asked me if I could tell him my name. This time, I did not hide my name. It is what it is. And I want my fellow countrymen to take me for what I am.

Today, the future of dissent and resistance is currently on thin ice with the subsequent arrests of students, activists, and civilians around the country. This also fills me with dread about the future of my country. The state must have crushed the place where the Shaheen Bagh happened by now, but the idea of Shaheen Bagh shall never fade as the movement fearlessly shouts out that 'resistance is the women'. How these women decided to dissent has several historical precedents – in the widows of Kashmir who protested against insurgency, in the women of Manipur who carried out nude protest against rape by the army men, in the *Mothers of Plaza de Mayo* who campaigned for their disappeared children.

As Arundhati Roy (1999) puts it, in her novel, *The Cost of Living*, 'To love. To be loved. To never forget your own insignificance. To never get used to the unspeakable violence and the vulgar disparity of life around you. To seek joy in the saddest places. To pursue beauty to its lair. To never simplify what is complicated or complicate what is simple. To respect strength, never power. Above all, to watch. To try and understand. To never look away. And never, never to forget.' That is precisely the lesson this movement gave me for life. As I go back to the times when I was subjected to judgements and reduced to my immediate identity as a Muslim woman in India, I realised that those experiences shaped my idea of dissent, marginalisation, justice, and empathy. My lack of privilege taught me what it feels to be politically disadvantaged in an unfair political discourse. And I would want my children to understand that an apolitical attitude is never a choice where there is injustice. Conversations around oppression, injustice, and falsehood deserve to be dealt with. Yet, you and me can be as 'Indian' as anybody else is.

5.2 Commentary

> Kill us; we will become ghosts and write
> of your killings, with all the evidence.
> You write jokes in court;
> We will write 'justice' on the walls.
> We will speak so loudly that even the deaf will hear.
> We will write so clearly that even the blind will read.
> You write 'injustice' on the earth;
> We will write 'revolution' in the sky.
> Everything will be remembered;
> Everything recorded.

Roger Waters, the Pink Floyd co-founder, read out the Indian poet and activist Aamir Aziz's English translation of the poem 'Sab Yaad Rakha Jayega' ('Everything Will Be Remembered') at a gathering in London in February 2020. Aamir Aziz wrote the verse in the context of the nationwide protests against the Citizenship Amendment Bill (CAA) in India, which seeks to desecularise the constitution by granting citizenship only to non-Muslim migrants escaping persecution. Along with rising attempts to silence activists who fight against the CAA, the Bill threatens future citizenship rights for Muslims in India in an already hostile environment. The very act of writing oppression reveals the fears, strengths, and anger under an oppressed regime. Historically, oppressed communities have challenged those in power against racism, homophobia, disenfranchisement, police brutality, and injustice through various written forms, ranging from letters, poetry, and pamphlets to song lyrics. Many of these written acts of resistance have been forced to disguise their intentions to protect the authors from persecution. But in my blog, I decided to sign my name, and say my name to the taxi driver in my story.

The very act of writing down the experience of oppression is one way that oppressed people can take charge of seeking their liberation. Writing the tragedy of being a minority in the state and the trauma associated with oppression can make one feel incredibly powerful. In the process, you learn to embrace your vulnerability, and confront your identity and existence within a systematically oppressive system. The power of writing was revolutionised in the 1960s by the Dalit Panthers, a group of writers considered as a low 'scheduled' caste, referred to as the 'untouchables'. They used poetry, fiction, and autobiography to document their rage from decades of humiliation, marginalisation, and brutal dehumanisation to assert their consciousness and identity through words. When the oppressed have come to be thought of as the 'other', or anti-national, as Muslims have now, writing down my Muslim name right below my experience in the blog itself becomes an act of resistance. To write is to resist. But writing also becomes an act to reconcile this other within us, break conventional rules of writing, and translate the years of structural and systematic dehumanisation to produce emancipatory theory. The assertion of identity, holding the very name that has been the reason for one's oppression for years – being unapologetically Muslim – while writing one's oppression is in itself a part of the process of reconciliation. Of course this takes work, but this is how writing can eventually give birth to meaningful resistance.

The choice to write oppression is also an act of faith, the belief that one day, these written words will evoke an understanding, empathy, and hope; that sharing fragments of banal everyday experiences of the oppressed will allow the readers to sense the totality of the oppression, the good, the evil, and the indifferent. Writings formed as part of a cultural resistance cannot be considered mere analytical texts; instead, the text also informs the masses about urgent political-cultural debates, the tactics of oppression, and the controlled authoritarian propaganda. And even more so, it is about finding common ground in the stories; it is not just you, there is more, and let the history attest for us. Ghassan Kanafani (2013 [1968]), the Palestinian journalist, activist, and critic, calls this cultural resistance 'no less valuable than armed resistance'. The Dalit literature, for example, is also a collective memory of oppression and a path for further political mobilisation as such kinds of literature are both political and politicised (Said, 1984). Individuals and communities often engage with resistance through remembering during conflicts. These narratives become testimonies to resist against the larger authoritarian narrative. As Amir Aziz wrote, *'Everything will be remembered; Everything recorded.'*

But as Hannah Arendt's (1963) exploration of the 'banality of evil' suggests, understanding how we think about the oppressor is not so simple. In analysing the trial of Adolf Eichmann, a Nazi military officer involved in the Holocaust, Arendt proposed that dreadful crimes such as the mass slaughter of the Jews in Germany are not often committed by sadists or sociopaths, but by sane ordinary beings. The idea is still considered to be widely controversial. Yet, the absolute mundanity and lack of demonic grandiosity in oppressors are essential for understanding the oppression against minorities in India. The Gujarat pogrom in the 2002 elections paved the way for the growing trivialisation and normalisation of lynchings of Muslims, where hundreds of Muslims were massacred or pushed into many of the state's ramshackled refugee camps. The state handed over the swords to the ordinary mass of Hindus, thereby establishing a shared, intense Hindu nationalist ideology amongst the ordinary mob, who believe that they deserve a tip of the hat for their victory in the pogrom. Just as historian Browning (1992) described in reference to the Holocaust, here we saw how ordinary men of lower socioeconomic class were made to believe that violence and hatred towards the oppressed were necessary to belong to the state.

V. D. Savarkar, one of the pioneers of Hindu nationalism, openly suggests that India should model its approach to its 'Muslim problem' just as Nazis tackled their 'Jewish problem' (Narayan, 2021), emphasising the deep-rooted ties between the far right in India and Europe. The Rashtriya Swayamsevak Sangh, a Hindu nationalist organisation, is reshaping Indian democracy through its vast network of educational and cultural discourses, mobilising everyday people through anti-Muslim slogans, lynchings, and pogroms on the Muslim community. The ruling party has successfully connected with Indian men from lower socioeconomic backgrounds by emphasising the 'humble' roots of nationalist prime minister Mr Narendra Modi as a Chaiwala (tea seller), winning the election polls amongst India's ordinary lower-class citizens. What is happening in India is exactly what Arendt warned against: evil has found a place in the world where violent actions are constantly justified and legitimised. Ordinary people are deployed to manipulate and manufacture hatred. The rampant crime against minorities in India is nothing unusual anymore. And so my cab driver who felt that all Muslims are *the same*, creatures walking around and spreading the virus, was probably one of many ordinary Indian men.

So then, how exactly do you approach a text when you are the oppressed yourself, and one has to confront the 'terrifyingly normal'? The ubiquitous experience of oppression might tempt us to conclude that there is nothing to discuss further on evil, but reducing the oppressor into a one-dimensional 'evil' figure on the page diminishes the immediacy and specificity of crucial historical context. In my ethnographic work on gender and migration of female domestic workers, I have become accustomed to linking personal experiences with larger social, economic, and political discourse. And here, with the cab driver, with the oppressor, I had to do the same. This time, with an ethnographic narrative of the oppressor – to describe the social conditions and social spaces which enable us to understand the stories of the oppressor. To distinguish between the traits belonging to each oppressor, including the multiplicity and diversity of the other, they needed to be demystified into an entity that could be easily comprehended.

This took an act of kindness. My craft of writing the oppressor primarily involved the attempt to demystify them by observing their nuances, in order to understand their story. The one-hour journey with the cab driver was also about sharing how our lives changed with the lockdown and how much he desired to educate his children. The hatred he had against Muslims was rather impersonal and abstract – a matter of following rules and consuming the majoritarian discourse. It lacked depth. Somewhere, he is an ordinary, banal being like me and you. He felt comfortable sharing his discomfort with me about Muslims. Probably because I was just like him: polite, cracked jokes as we talked, and conformed pretty well to his expectations of how a 'good' person acts. It was probably my curiosity and willingness to engage in an open dialogue with the cab driver's perspective on his perception of Muslims that compelled me to write my story with kindness in the first place. Crucially, the act of kindness while writing the oppressor does not intend to downplay the evil; someooone does not engage in politics unless their cause has a future, has faith. Instead, the process intends to understand the complexity of the evil, dig deeper to find the causes, striking powerful chords into the multiple forms of evil and how it is practised amongst different levels of society. This process can be a way forward to advance the understanding of radical evil. Then, the question is, will I remain an ordinary, banal being after I uttered my name to him?

This is why, at the same time, I acknowledge that kindness while writing one's oppressor comes from a certain kind of privilege. As per the popular analysis in the *Pedagogy of the Oppressed* by Freire (1970), the duty of the oppressed is to realise the humanity which the oppressor denies them, eventually liberating the oppressor and the oppressed. But we must not expect the same from every oppressed entity as they represent their oppressor through the act of writing. Kindness may not always be possible while writing the oppressor. When the oppressed write about their humiliation and shame, their narratives and experiences, the oppressed have the right to choose how they perceive their oppression/oppressor – whether it be perverted, sadistic, shallow, or banal. The most authentic understanding of the oppressor is the lens through which the subjugated entity chooses to translate their oppression.

But in whatever multiple ways people choose to write the oppressor, life writings of the oppressed can eventually assist in locating the broader historical and political routes of shame, humiliation, disgust, and social justice. Years from now, the documentation of diverse oppressors, the ordinary and the extraordinary, will be written down through the lens of oppressed Muslims, opening discussions around the world on what it will take to cease the endless destruction of the minority community's capacity to exist with dignity.

6 Writing as Rioting: The Resistance of the Object by Sibo Kanobana

6.1 Blog Post

POSTED 29 JUNE 2020

Who Is Not on the List? Navigating White Academia

Figure 6.1 Exam entrance during Covid-19. Author's image.

'Your name is not on the list', she said, 'I can't let you in'. She wasn't unfriendly but made it clear that I wasn't supposed to be there, that I should leave.

A few weeks ago I got an email from the head of my department at university asking for volunteers to invigilate the exams. Due to Covid-19, exams had to be organised differently. Instead of one auditorium with one hundred students supervised by two or three academics, the group had to be split in four and spread over four different auditoriums. Consequently, there was a need for more invigilators, and I volunteered to help.

I was assigned to a location, but when I arrived the people in front of the building responsible for registering the students and distributing facemasks said they couldn't let me in. I said I was here with Mark Van der Steen,[5] that he was also an invigilator, and that he should already be inside. She took a look at her list again and said: 'There is no Mark Van der Steen either, sorry, I think you are at the wrong location.'

I started to doubt myself, so I took my phone and checked my emails. Did I miss something? Did I forget to read a last urgent email? Or did I come on the wrong day? Was it yesterday or rather next week? I started to get stressed,

---

[5] This is a pseudonym.

scrolling through my emails and using the search function to find any mails I could have missed, went through my spam. Nothing. I couldn't find any other emails than the communication in which I responded and confirmed that I would be there. I showed the lady my email, but she wasn't interested. She repeated: 'Sorry, you're not on the list, you can't get in.'

She had other things to do as students started to arrive. I didn't have Mark's phone number, so I sent him an email with my phone, telling him I was in front of the building but that they wouldn't let me in. I withdrew myself from the entrance and started to think while standing on the sidewalk. What now? I returned to my emails, searching for my mistake but couldn't find it, when suddenly after a few minutes Mark stood behind me and said, 'Hi Sibo, come on in'.

I was surprised. Where did he come from so suddenly? 'I was already in the auditorium', he said, 'I arrived fifteen minutes ago. I just opened my computer and saw your email'. 'But your name is not on the list', I said, 'How did you get in?' He didn't know, he didn't even know there was a list, they just let him in, he said. I was puzzled, so I went to the lady with him and said, 'Well this is Mark Van der Steen, my colleague with whom I will supervise the exam in auditorium A1'. She looked at her list and seemed a little confused or embarrassed, and then said to Mark, 'So, he is with you?', while pointing at me with her pen. Mark said yes and that was it. It was confirmed. It was all good now. I could get in.

I was perplexed. What happened? I couldn't stop thinking: 'But Mark is not on the list either. Why did they let him in? Why is he a trustworthy source of information for letting me in? Why does he have to confirm that I'm okay while she doesn't know him either? Why did she let him in in the first place? Why didn't she ask his name? He's not on the list and is still not on the list, even after he came to fetch me.'

I didn't say anything, but I was kind of pissed off. I didn't show it though. I am a nice guy. I knew that being angry wouldn't help much. But I kept on thinking about what happened. Why was I treated that way, and Mark wasn't? Mark and I are the same age, we're both fathers, we're both middle class, we both have facial hair, we both speak fluent Dutch, we both have the same educational background. So, what has happened here? Is it our bodies? I'm taller and slimmer than Mark and he's balding while I have long hair, dreadlocks actually. And yes, maybe it's that. The dreadlocks. Maybe my father was right all along. I should cut my hair, and wear a suit and tie. Just not to scare people. Because, you see, I am black. The brown skin, mixed race type. The fashionable type. But still black. Still a threat. Mark, however, is white.

But thinking that is really problematic. I mean how could race matter here, in this progressive university? We're in Western Europe, in a rich, clean, well-organised, liberal university town. The local mantra is that racism is relative, that if you speak the local language, all doors will open for you. Well, in this case, the door stayed closed. Even if I did speak Dutch perfectly, if that is even possible. I speak Dutch with the local accent, the local well-educated version of Dutch.

So, I keep on thinking, wouldn't it be short-sighted of me to label this woman and her colleagues racists? Race can't be the thing here. I just wasn't on the list. It's a bureaucratic matter. An administrative mistake. Moreover, we are in a predominately white town. Very few people with my appearance live here, even less work at university. And this university brands itself as a progressive institution. Can I blame this mistake on racism? I think so, but I don't want to. To protect myself. Because if I would have dared to say there was something racist going on, that I demanded an apology for the mix up, that wouldn't be constructive. That would have made me an angry black man. You don't want anyone to think you're angry *and* black. That's dangerous. Moreover, I would be made responsible for the situation escalating. I would be framed as oversensitive. Another black stereotype. So why bother? Just keep silent.

I didn't say a thing. I didn't make a scene. I focused on my privileges. I didn't have a cop's knee on my neck, after all. I wasn't going to die. I could breathe. So I didn't ask why she didn't refuse Mark entrance if he's not on her list. I didn't confront her. Who cares. It's not my problem, it's hers. She was just doing her job, right?

I asked Mark, though, what he thought had gone on. I was disappointed as there was no outrage on his part. He didn't seem puzzled. We were both not on the list, because we were both replacing a professor, so he guessed that the professor's name would be on the list and therefore not ours. I agreed, but it didn't make sense. 'Why did she let *you* in, and not me? Why did *you* have to confirm that I was an invigilator? What kind of power do *you* have that I haven't? White power?'

I didn't say these things, I didn't want to make him feel bad. White power? Seriously? I kept that to myself. My past experiences told me that making white people feel uncomfortable about race is not solving problems. At least, not in the moment. I focus on the good intentions, ignore the bad effects it has on me. The insecurity, the self-doubt. I relativise. I tell myself that's what happens when you're one of the few black people in a white world. Of course she thinks I might be up to no good. That's what people of colour are mediatised for. That's our specialty. Being up to no good.

Still, what Mark said didn't explain a thing. We were both not on the list. We were eight invigilators spread over four locations to supervise one exam for one professor. His analysis didn't address my question. However, I'm a well-behaved law-abiding citizen, I didn't say anything, I didn't want to go over this again, I didn't want to cause unease. They were all acting and talking with the best intentions, I assumed. I was being complicated. I felt insecure. I said, 'Thank you', to the lady and I thanked Mark, my white saviour. And I promised myself I would try to forget this episode as quickly as possible.

But I didn't forget. The rollercoaster of news about Black Lives Matter and the effects it had worldwide made me aware that I had to tell this story. Until now, I always chose to dismiss the importance of such personal experiences. After all, most people weren't intentionally racist. I kept my anger for the fascists, not for the nice people who had learned to assume that I could be a threat. It wasn't their fault. It was the system. I told myself this wasn't racism, it was ignorance. However, the pain and distress it caused made me realise that ignorance *is* racism.

I've been talking about race for decades, but always in theoretical, historical, and sociological terms. Never about myself, never about my experience. It seemed impossible, it wasn't objective, it was anecdotal, and it was traumatising. However, through my ethnographic work I came to learn that society, history, and theory are there, in these little everyday interactions, and that if we want to talk about racism we need to look at these everyday interactions to understand how racism works. Even if my current research project is not centred around my personal experiences, it taught me clearly that racism is not a matter of bad individuals, it's indeed a systemic problem. Racism is not this specific lady's problem, not Mark's problem, not my problem. It's *our* problem. And if I keep silent about it, I am part of the problem. I could have made that point at the time it happened, but my point wouldn't have landed well. I would be an angry black man and thus a public danger. I would be overreacting. This blog seemed to be one of the limited ways I had to break the silence without harming myself. Still, it's me who has to revisit something I'd rather forget. In the moment, Mark with his power might have been able to achieve more than I could. I had to control my outrage, to protect myself. But where was his outrage? Why didn't he call out what happened? Of course, it is not his personal responsibility, it's not just his problem. Again, it is *our* problem. And as long as we don't address it as such I'm afraid that we will never be able to change racism's systemicity.

6.2 Commentary

> Black man gotta lot a problems
> But they don't mind throwing a brick
> White people go to school
> Where they teach you how to be thick
> From *White Riot* (The Clash, 1977)

I wanted to tell a personal story, which I thought was worth sharing because of its political implications. I wanted to resonate, but felt that the personal had no legitimate place in my academic writing. So I wrote a blog post. I've actually never understood language as a collection of prescribed signs with a discrete meaning. That kind of writing has never been satisfactory, because my experience told me that words are not things; they are where invention is brought into existence (Fanon, 1952, p. 179). I will try to tell you what that means for me and how writing is a part of my revolt against a world that objectifies me.

Like many teenagers, I used to write teenage poetry. No love poems though. I was searching for my identity. Yes, identity, for lack of a better word. I found inspiration in biology, school books about the scientific study of life, with texts that appeared dead to me. I copied the definition of a cell, but subverted the phrases on the white page. I wrote as a riot full of rage, transformed scientific jargon into a story to be told on a stage. Biology appeared somehow reductionist to me, and even if biology's etymology reveals that it's a discipline that speaks of life, biology didn't mention what seemed fundamental to my life: passion, pleasure, pain, doubt, commitment, relation, hate, love. The story that biology told about us seemed devoid of life, constrained to the dissected factual. But we are never just a cluster of facts; we are poetic too. And poetic knowledge is necessary when scientific knowledge fails to recognise our complexity, our ambivalences and vulnerabilities, our relationalities (Césaire, 1945, p. 157). This is where writing has to riot, to destroy categorisation, and to bring the poetic back to life. The scientific knowledge that objectifies us, that makes us into things and discrete objects, is a form of colonisation, because 'colonisation = "thingifi-cation"' (Césaire, 1950, p. 42). I reject being thingified, to thingify anyone or anything, and rather want to explore how our humanity can be amplified.

In light of all these crises we face – ecological, political, economic, moral, mental, demographic – I want to make a case for writing as a subversion, because I see these crises engendered by a scientific logic that sterilises. Of course, we are also flesh and bones, we are sometimes sick and cold, we change from young to old, but we are so much more that hasn't been told as part of the essential knowledge we should hold. No, our institutions of knowledge produc-tion want us to tell stories presented as *no stories at all*, disinfected scientific discourses devoid of idiosyncrasies. The facts. But who are the people who are looking for a factually scientifically validated answer about who they are? Who are the people who want to sanitise their being? It has never been me. I'd rather make it all dirty.

That's when I started to write rap lyrics. French was my language of choice in the mix. Then I rapped to slam. No rhymes are necessary, just rhythm. Dutch,

Swahili, English, Lingala, French. A wide linguistic prism. I could not choose a language; I could not choose a genre. I had too many. I had to slam it all down. 'Writing [as] a constant disruption of the means of semantic production, all the time . . . I don't see any reason to try to avoid that. I'd rather see a reason to try to accentuate that . . . not in the interest of obfuscation but in the interest of precision' (Fred Moten in Wallace, 2018). It may sound paradoxical, but messy explanations are usually more precise. Closer to the living truth of our lives. That's where my blackness becomes a blur. A colour that is not a colour *at all*. The absence of colour, actually. Black identity like an oxymoron. An identity that rejects I-dentity. Blackness doesn't mind to improvise and disturb, to throw a brick, to ask who we are. My blog post might have been like that brick, a brick I threw out in the world. Colleagues who had never read my academic writings read the blog and I felt their embarrassment. My writing had created discomfort. Good. The riot had started. And the goal wasn't to claim my blackness, no, but to deflect the whiteness around me. We're indeed never just this or that. Our identity has no intrinsic features, because we are an amalgamation of our relations and I refuse the racialised, write as a riot to forge genuine human affiliations.

Who we are appears to be 'located where disruption and creation meet' (Moten, 2003, p. 213). Think about the breakbeat, think into the break. It's there that we see a glimpse of who we are. The difficulty then lies not in new ideas, but in escaping the old ones. Hence, there is a difference between having an identity and grounding your complete being *in* I-dentity, encapsulating an essence devoid of interaction. Identity then is an icon with which I con myself. That's when exclusion comes in, that's when we lose the relationality of being human; we become things with inherent characteristics, things that are *exclusive*. That's why we need to embrace the necessity to riot linguistically, to challenge the silence of scientific language. Indeed, who we are is not to be found in a birth certificate, a passport, or phenotype. Are you on the list? I guess I wasn't. Even the professor's email didn't do the trick. I needed to throw a brick, because the lady basically said: Sir, this is the border. As far as I can see, your type is not supposed to be here, and do not contest me, I have work to do. Please don't come near. The border is then the end, the terminal, the finish, the extermination. That's when 'race is . . . not the beginning of humanity but its end' (Arendt, 1951, p. 157). Race then doesn't just dehumanise the racially marked, but denies our interconnectedness and deprives us *all* of our humanity (Gilroy, 2001, p. 15); it destroys us all mentally (Fanon, 1952, p. 42).

Being human is thus no theory, but a praxis (McKittrick, 2015) of interaction in sounds, smells, touch, music, dance, poetry. A praxis that resides in the truthful impossibility to fit in. Writing can be a praxis of being human, of creating meaning and speaking to the reader, of forging a connection. That's what I tried with a blog post, writing as a way to resist objectification and to lay out what it does with me. I expect that whoever has experienced being reduced to *what* they are, rather than being recognised for *who* they are, identifies with the distress in the story. Hence, 'Agree not merely to the right of difference but, carrying this further, agree also to the right to opacity' (Glissant, 1997, p. 190). Because you too are full of ambiguities and contradictions. Nobody is just white, just black, just cis, just trans, just old, just gay, just whatever category scientific knowledge has imposed on us that reduces us to quantitative data that inform inhuman policies. We need stories.

We are hungry for billions of different stories, and writing is a technology we can apply to discover our own 'non-totalisable intense multiplicity' (Deleuze & Guattari, 1987, p. 58). To write is then to riot because every act of creation is first an act of destruction. Indeed, it seems that the numbers, charts, statistics, and lists have made us lose our imagination. As a result, today it's easier to imagine the end of the world than to imagine the end of capitalist accumulation (Fisher, 2009). That's the danger of the single story (Adichie, 2009), and that's why '*you have to tell your own story simultaneously as you hear and respond to the stories of others*' (Alexander, 2007, p. 129). Language is a tool for that. Ethnographic writing can then be an unruly act, and listening is part of that. Then you react. Because we know we're so much more than whatever can be put on paper and defined as exact. So, use language, not as a thing you can grasp, but as a place where you can create meaning and interact. The riot may be a first step, the necessary poetic hack of all that is labelled scientific fact.

7 Finding Places to Disrupt by Hannah Cowan

7.1 Blog Post

POSTED 16 MAY 2020

We Will Not Tolerate Any Form of Abuse: Reconstructing Disability Assessments and Surveillance Post-Covid

Figure 7.1 The Disability Assessment Centre.

This blog was written in collaboration and conversation with a friend, who would prefer to remain anonymous.

'We will not tolerate any form of abuse . . .' I started reading the sign in the waiting room of the Centre for Health and Disability Assessments. Back before the Covid-19 lockdown I was waiting with a friend for an appointment which would determine whether she was still eligible for Employment and Support Allowance. MAXIMUS is the most recent company contracted to carry out these assessments, which determine what money people can claim to support their disability needs.

I carried on reading the sign:

'We have a duty of care to both our customers and our staff. Most of our customers are polite and understanding. We will treat our customers with respect. We will not tolerate:

• Threats
• Verbal abuse

- Assault
- Harassment
- Racism

We will be strong in our actions, including prosecution, against anyone responsible for abuse.'

Had the centre experienced violence before? I looked around and saw people quietly waiting in the chairs bordering the room. There was a woman with crutches waiting with what appeared to be her husband and daughter. There was a man in his twenties who smelt a little of booze and was quietly twiddling his thumbs while his social worker sat next to him reading a newspaper. And there was me and my friend waiting for her assessment on her back condition, which has taken her in and out of hospital and in need of carers in the home for years. The most violent thing to me in that room was the poster itself, acting as a forceful and permanent threat to anyone who stepped out of line. The security guard by the door and the insecurity of everyone's position made the power dynamics quite clear.

During the Covid-19 lockdown, I have seen numerous activists and graffiti artists saying we cannot go back to 'normal'. That we should use this sudden breakdown of social relations as a moment for radical change; to reconstruct the world we want to come back to. This is sometimes hard to contemplate when we have seen inequalities entrench themselves further with lockdown, as described in my own and Alfonso's previous posts. But one way in which Covid-19 has brought about a *decrease* of surveillance is through the suspension of any disability assessments during lockdown. It is momentarily assumed that those that ask for help need it. The insecurity in that room previous to the moment of rupture in which I write this, was because everyone waiting was reliant on the assessment to justify their needs for financial help. Help to pay for food and rent when they cannot work, and to pay for carers who may need to help with getting up out of bed, or daily tasks such as the shopping and cleaning. These assessments were introduced in the UK for everyone needing disability benefits to distinguish what one national television programme called the 'Saints and Scroungers'; to ensure no one was faking their illness to thieve financial benefits from the welfare state. Unfortunately, the only way of being a saint in that TV show was if you were living in stress and poverty by not claiming anything from the state. Everyone in that room, therefore, who were all claiming money from the state, was a suspected scrounger. Assumed guilty.

As we were waiting, two young men came rushing in, probably about twenty or twenty-one years old. They were both in surfer-style clothing and were clearly quite athletic given the panicked entrance they'd just made. Not all disabilities are visible. They hurried up to the woman on the desk, my friend said she could feel their fear. 'So sorry we're late, we got stuck in traffic!' one of them managed to get the words out while catching his breath. I wasn't surprised some people were late, given that this vital centre was hidden from view in the backstreets of a town many had to travel miles to get to (including us). Anyway, surely a disability assessment should make allowances given that anything from mental health, to learning difficulties, to physical health might impact people's ability to manage timekeeping in the style of a productive worker.

'What's the name?' the woman asked, unmoved by the situation ... 'Well, looking at this you're ten minutes late and seeing as we're running behind, we're not going to be able to see you – you're going to have to rearrange.' 'Ahh really?!' they asked, still trying to catch their breath. The two guys looked at each other. No words, no retort. They walked out; shoulders slumped. Defeated. I watched as they lit up a cigarette the other side of the glass door; exasperated and powerless. My friend and I looked at each other – her appointment was half an hour ago and we were still waiting. It didn't help that they only had one assessment room on the ground floor and no lift in the building. My friend was using me as a prop, unable to sit in the chairs provided, struggling with the pain. There's no way these guys missed their slot. MAXIMUS are allowed to be late, but those coming to get assessed are not.

Only a few weeks ago the centre cancelled on us at the last minute. We were waiting for the car which they had arranged to take my friend to the centre. A request for transport is the only evidence they would take from the doctor involved in my friend's care. But as the minutes ticked by, we too started to become fearful that we wouldn't make it on time. If you're late, or you have to rearrange your appointment more than once, you are deemed 'non-compliant' and your case gets penalised. Two years ago, my friend couldn't attend, as she was bedbound, and they stopped paying her a few months later; without notice. That was another frightening and arduous time.

Back in the present, we were frantically phoning round all the offices. Going round in circles. It was a Saturday and many of the numbers we tried went straight to answer machines. Finally, a human being. The assessment was cancelled, no car was coming. They just forgot to tell us.

This might seem dramatic. But the preparation for the assessment is more than just making sure someone has booked the day off work to accompany you. It is the kind of mental preparation you need to defend the income that is paying your rent, your food, your care. My friend was hyper aware of the media reports and whistleblowers describing the ways Atos, the previous company in charge of these assessments, had been trying to catch people out. And the memories of my friend's previous assessments weren't encouraging.

They watch you as soon as you get out of the taxi, she told me. That's why the walkway is there. Cars can't go right up to the entrance. Instead there is a walkway painted in yellow on the tarmac with a perfectly proportioned stick man painted down the middle, helpfully illustrating how one should stride to the entrance. When she had to go to a tribunal previously, to defend her need for care, she found out that when she was physically struggling to be polite and not cause a fuss, to open doors and pull out chairs, this was 'evidence' used against her. They never asked if these actions caused her pain or if she felt able to repeat them. It is just a tick box. And worse than the surveillance, last time they caused her immediate, physical, pain. They wanted to check her reflexes by tapping her knee. They tapped the first knee and her whole leg and lower back went into spasm. She put her hand up, and asked the nurse to stop, clearly in pain. The nurse ignored her and tapped the other one anyway, sending another, this time unexpected, shock up her spine. Neither the spasms, nor the pain, were recorded in her report, and my friend was deemed fit for work. It took the stress of a tribunal to have her benefits reinstated.

Figure 7.2 Generic able man painted on the walkway.

The focus of this monetary benefit, as the title 'Employment and Support Allowance' suggests, has become one of getting people back into work. There is some work my friend could and wants to do. But the economy isn't made for someone with the unpredictability of her condition. Where she can be bedbound for days, weeks, or months at a time, and the medication she takes can cause temporary cognitive and neurological problems. If she even went for an interview, would they understand? Fear and guilt are the oscillating constants, my friend tells me. She feels guilty that she needs the benefits and her carers, but she is fearful that if she tries to do a little work, they will stop her benefits completely. And if an employer isn't happy with her long stretches of illness, she would have to reapply for benefits all over again. When she is lucky enough to have some good days, to venture outside of her living room, it doesn't come without the guilt and fear. Would someone report her? She recalls overhearing someone in the pub: 'Look at her wasting our taxpayer's money, she doesn't even look sick.' She's aware that CCTV footage from supermarkets and public spaces, as well as social media images, can get used to build a case against her. She is always, potentially, being watched.

You've got to put it on a bit, people were advising my friend beforehand. To make sure she got the support they knew she needed. But she didn't want to do that. She wouldn't dream of going outside without her usual attire. A dress, make-up, and some boots or sandals carefully selected from the paediatric shoe shop. She wants to be polite, strain herself to help others. She wants to keep her dignity. But after spending some time with her preparing for this assessment, I realised she didn't need to 'put it on'. Rather, it was a process of taking off the act; the mask she puts on in public to hide the pain, and show everyone that she's okay. Taking off the mask is an emotional process in itself, and one which causes unacknowledged pain and duress, especially in front of strangers.

Back in the assessment centre we finally got called, our turn. The assessment nurse was stern that we were not allowed to record the meeting but assured us that she would not do anything to cause harm. The interview was fast-paced and as soon as the assessor had figured out where to place my friend, which box to tick, she moved on to the next question. There was no time for my friend to process the questions, elaborate, and make sure she gave all the information. The nurse didn't want to see the huge folder of daily care notes we had carefully packed as evidence – she said she didn't want to know what the carers spread on her toast every morning. We had to push for her to glance at the daily recordings of pain levels and photocopy them as evidence. As we got to the end, I could see my friend getting more nervous in anticipation of a re-run of the physical exam.

'Oh no I don't need to do a physical examination with you, I can tell that you're not well. It's just if people come in saying they've got a bit of a bad back.'

This decisive phrase both did and didn't make everything feel okay.

There was of course a great relief that there was not going to be a potentially harmful physical examination. But the immediacy of that 'benefit scrounger' figure made it clear they were constantly on the look-out for that back that's not quite bad enough. While they say they acknowledge people can have good and bad days, the day of the assessment has really got to be a specific kind of a day. A day that's good enough to make it to the appointment, but one that's bad enough for them to be convinced you need support.

When my friend finally got the letter, she found she had a reduction in financial support. She didn't get enough points. Ironically, she ended up in hospital not long after.

I looked back up at the poster in the waiting room: *We will not tolerate any form of abuse*. The only form of abuse I saw was the abuse of how people with disabilities are being treated and assessed by the benefits system and the contracted assessment centres. Not only causing physical harm at times but forcing people to strip themselves of their coping mechanisms, and be denied their dignity and a good life, while living with a disability. The poster is just another form of abuse – putting the potential for violence back onto those in need of support.

When talking to my friend about the world we would want to reconstruct post-Covid, it isn't about cancelling or getting rid of these assessments. It's the abuse we will not tolerate. Could surveillance be done with care? We're still stuck on this one. Where many conditions that affect people's lives are constantly changing, and unpredictable, my friend suggests it would be comforting to know that support can be reactive to changing situations. These assessments could be about understanding needs. Not catch-you-out assessments. They could be about bringing all the different forms of expertise together – from carers, doctors, physios, surgeons, and the patient themselves. To understand where support is needed, and necessarily therefore, where it isn't. Finding ways to help people live a comfortable and good life. One which supports people with work where this is possible and valuable to them. And one which makes people feel justified and worth the support they receive. At a time where surveillance of disease is becoming necessary to move us out of lockdown, I have to ask again: can surveillance be done with care?

7.2 Commentary

It took me a long time to finish this blog post – it wasn't the easiest writing experience. Looking back, this was partly because I was writing about a very oppressive situation, where it felt like some all-encompassing, inescapable structure was weighing down on me and my friend from above. The world closed in. There are these sociological images of how society is structured with the individual in the middle, then rainbow arches around them labelled 'social and community networks', 'work', and so on, until you reach the most outer and totalising one of them all: 'general socio-economic, cultural, and environmental conditions' (see Dahlgreen & Whitehead, 1991). It felt like we were trapped by the cultural and bureaucratic systems put in place to continually reduce disability welfare payments, and make everyone experiencing disability a potential 'benefit cheat'.

I started writing soon after I had spent the day with my friend who was getting sick from the physical and mental stress of preparing for a catch-you-out assessment. Seeing just how much the process was hurting her made me incredibly angry. Don't get me wrong, it took time for the in-action moments to turn into anger. Twenty-four hours or so. It was the kind of anger that if expressed in the assessment centre itself, you would probably be told you were abusive, be arrested, and never receive any welfare payments again. Anger has tactfully been coded simultaneously 'uncivil' and alongside various oppressed groups – 'angry woman', 'angry black man', 'angry working classes' – by those who have the privilege to remain calm. Anger is of course a reasonable response to violence and oppression, but if it gets expressed, the oppression just doubles down again to keep people in line – violence (read anger) will not be tolerated. To be fair, on my part, it was also the kind of anger that perhaps isn't so useful in those immediate moments of care. For me, and everyone else in that room, the anger had to be suppressed, bottled up, at least for a time.

But when the anger rose, it came intensely for days. I had to do something with that energy. So I went to sit in the corner of a quiet pub with my laptop, slowly turning rarrgghhh emotions into actual words. I hadn't started writing intentionally as a blog post; it wasn't meant for publication. Writing was initially just a way of processing, working through the anger. Coding it into language, transforming one energy into another as my fingers typed.

By processing anger, I don't mean I reasoned *away* my anger; I'm not suggesting we calm down. No, this is not a way of rationalising anger, but rather emoting knowledge. I started this process by holding the anger in *closer* to get to know it better: what are the injustices going on here and how precisely are they occurring? As I wrote, the nouns located actors, objects, things, and the verbs identified the relations between them. Injustices were no longer in a cloud over my head but down here by my feet, within grasping, touching, distance. I could see, smell, hear them. I could feel the textures, the ways in which people feel compelled into movement. Then, the anger needed to be distributed. Not channelled, but carefully allocated, attaching it to the specific practices, people, things, and scenarios that have created the injustices in the world around me.

Because we can hate the monolith, that structure that seems to be pinning us down. Shout at it, go on – it's useful and therapeutic, directs that painful energy out of us and in the general direction of where it belongs. But we can be in danger of misdirecting it if we don't first hold the anger close and write in ethnographic detail to work out the seemingly banal actions from which it has manifested. Or worse, we can be in danger of shouting into an ether where our anger dissipates, and everything and everyone responsible shrugs their shoulders and claims there's nothing they can do about it. Writing helps to work out exactly where this angry energy does belong.

So as I wrote, and rewrote, I began to break down the monolith. These injustices didn't happen because of some 'general socio-economic, cultural, and environmental conditions'. These injustices happened because one nurse physically injured my friend, another didn't listen, only concerned with ticking boxes. A receptionist didn't try to do anything when someone was very obviously distressed about being late. Another didn't phone to inform us when an appointment was cancelled. Of course, some might suggest that these people were acting within a constrained system, but this system, these conditions, are also posters on walls, abled silhouettes painted on pathways, drives blocked with bollards so you can't drive up to the door. Someone had to write and print that poster about abuse, and then pin it to the wall. Another painted the silhouette. Others decided to set up a company which would make profit out of reducing people's disability payments, signed the contract, and decided to call the company MAXIMUS, a gladiator name meaning 'the strongest, the biggest'. Some TV producers, script writers, presenters, and everyone else involved in the production of a TV series, made a show called *Saints and Scroungers*. The point is that systems, structures, conditions aren't just inescapable bonds. They are made up of people, things, and the relations we make between them. These people and things are all affecting each other, riling each other up to justify and normalise worse actions, and the whole mess gets called 'the system'.

Crucially, this writing practice doesn't only help us identify the banal making of inequality, but also enables us to find places to make change; places for banal resistance. If injustices are made by banal relations between people and things, then we can severe these relations, or remake them if we wish. Resistance is accessible to each and every one of us. Turn the other way, do nothing. Or do something else, change your focus. Take down the poster from the wall. It only need be banal. Resist. Nothing much really; we swallow whole tapestries but we can reweave stories before passing them on by changing just a stitch.

Sometimes when you're writing the intricacies of events you can identify banal yet renegade actions which have potential to do good, or at least better, for the oppressed. I managed to find some of these instances in my PhD work where, for example, some healthcare workers insisted on enabling vulnerable patients to stay another night in the hospital they were going to be made to leave to maintain targets (Cowan, 2021). But I couldn't find much in the way of banal resistance in my short time at the disability assessment centre, except for from SARS-CoV-2 which stopped the appointments altogether. Sometimes people's imaginations have been so quelled by what is seemingly possible in the present they find ways to justify or ignore the ways in which their banal actions create injustice. So other times, you have to first imagine alternative forms of banal doings to even possibilise them in action. So here, I decided to think of ethnography as what Levitas (2013) calls the archaeology of the present; a way of excavating the ways in which banal actions lead to injustice. We can then use this to reimagine alternatives, reinscribe these very same actions to find a way out, open up the cracks.

But here I got stuck for another reason. Writing started as a process, but as soon as I began to edit, shape it for an audience, something started to feel wrong. I stopped writing. I felt in danger of being an exploitative researcher, making capital out of a story that wasn't mine to tell. I didn't pick it up again until, mid-conversation with my friend, she said 'you could write one of your blogs about this!'. I was so concerned about being a colonial anthropologist attempting to capture a story that I hadn't realised there was a flip side. Sometimes people want to share their stories, and they want a hand to tell it well. I'd forgotten that writing is also an art form, a skill, that needs to be honed through practice. And even so, it is my story too, my friend reassured me. And so, we got to work thinking about how we experienced and how we would make the story together. We alternated between talking and me going away to write, sharing the text, and rewriting if I hadn't quite got something right, or something else emerged through spoken word.

Thinking through the words together added to both the story and our lives off the page. For my friend, she tells me, the process helped her find her anger. Where I had the freedom to be angry, find the space to let the anger rise, my friend is stuck surrounded, like a rabbit in the headlights of many cars continually telling her that her quality of life has little worth to them. This prevents her fighting *or* flighting; there isn't enough space. But the collective storytelling process allowed my friend to see it through a bystander's eyes and reclaim her anger-knowledge. For me, on the other hand, my friend prodded, cajoled me out of my own enthralled position-ality that had been ingrained through my academic training. I thought that it was brilliant that all the appointments had stopped. No more surveillance. But through our many conversations, my friend challenged the sociology-101 script that surveillance is always a terrible exercise of power. As my friend suggested, you can't care properly without it. To care is a form of *looking* after, monitoring, checking up on, surveying. It wasn't the surveillance which was wrong. It was the way in which it was done, and the outcomes that were being focused on. As we imagined new worlds, we wanted people to accommodate; remove the bollards, understand delays. But we also tried to imagine a world where the nurses continued to keep track, collaborated with other health professionals, and made sure everyone had the money and resources appropriate to their changing needs. At this point we invited the reader into our imaginary exercise, asked them to think banal utopias with us: can surveillance be done with care?

For me, the point of ethnography is not only for the story, the end result. The point is also in the process. Writing helps us unravel and identify the practices, the relations, that need to change. This was a particularly complex set of relations to unpack, and with a name like MAXIMUS it's hard not to get startled by the sheer size of the operation, the numbers of complicit people involved. But writing – ethnography – can help us work through it, make inequalities more proximal, and the mechanisms that create them more banal. Crucially, to find good places to disrupt in these mechanisms, we first have to claim our emotions, hold them up close and then share our anger through writing, through storytelling: attach it to the right things, direct it in the right places. The process of writing, extended to the conversations that went into it, allowed me and my friend to locate places for change together. Of course, this is an ongoing process. You can't solve oppression everywhere in a day, a blog, or a conversation. The world we are working with is constantly shifting, changing. The writing is never done.

8 Conclusion: Forming a Banal Resistance by Hannah Cowan

Through these sections we, as editors and authors, have illustrated how attending to banal inequalities enables us to make visible the often hidden, mundane, and everyday production and experience of inequalities. The stories we have shared are of course fabricated in particular ways, and so we have also attempted to reveal and critique our writing practices; our choices, reflections, strategies, tools, and tactics, but also our agendas, intentions, and emotions that we mobilise to craft and shape the stories we intend to tell. In this final part of the Element, we, as editors, wish to elaborate more on what we consider to be the most important aspect of our writing practice. Namely how, through writing banal inequalities, we can attempt to craft and share stories which disrupt. Through these writing practices we have been able to think with and develop what we call banal resistance.

The first way in which we form this banal resistance is simply in the documentation of alternative stories to the hegemonic histories of the present, which have long imposed unproblematised collective memories and celebrated histories. At times just the act of making a record of events, and even signing your name to it if you can find the strength, can problematise relations and events that are seemingly benign to those not attuned to oppression. But by proliferating new stories which problematise people's everyday doings, and putting a spotlight on people's daily experiences of violence and discomfort, we also hope to denormalise and reject the present, and delegitimise the everyday practices which create these situations. We make clear that the relations of power and oppression which constitute inequality are not pregiven, nor necessary. As so many writers (especially anthropologists) have made clear by documenting alternative relations around the world, social inequalities do not have to be the way they are (Graeber, 2004). Rather, inequalities are constituted by complex relations between human, non-human, and material, the present and the past, and the here and there; they are the product of complex and dynamic circumstances, decisions, and indecisions.

This is why we have resisted the cultural imperative to simplify relations, to label these interactions with isms. Our microphysical approach to storytelling is not only important for us to be able to point to the where, when, why, and how inequality is constituted and perpetuated. Writing the material circumstances of our stories – the objects, environments, and historical relations – is crucial, Alfonso suggests, to demonstrate the material inequalities rather than simply speculate about what is going on in people's heads to make an emotionally gratifying story for all to feel. It enables us to attend to the ways in which each and every one of us can be both oppressed and the oppressor – and even, as

Amal suggests, show kindness towards our oppressors (including the oppressor in each of us) in order to gain a better understanding of what is going on in the world. We also resist the need to make tidy endings to our stories and clean up the messy intersectional relations in the world. Our stories have to deal with many, sometimes conflicting, sides – a kaleidoscope of shifting constellations. As Natassia suggests, sometimes it is better to hold the difficult relations in place for both writer and reader to see together. The forms of ethnographic writing we introduce in this Element allow us then not only to denormalise and delegitimise inequality, but also to free ourselves of untouchable isms, and to identify and deconstruct the conditions under which banal inequalities are produced. Here, we want to make it clear that at times it can be (and has to be because of more entrapping oppressive situations) enough just to document, to understand, to explain inequality, but also that this, as Levitas (2013) suggests, is the first disruptive step which then enables us to imagine alternative futures in which we all could live.

The second way in which we disrupt, then, is through reconstructing as well as deconstructing the world in our fabricated texts – to tread that line between fact and fiction and bring new possibilities into the world. We agree with Will and Sibo in thinking that this reimagination and remaking of our futures should include the subversion of the genres and categories that we use to write and make sense of our social worlds. Rather than reinscribe unequal relations into the years ahead, we suggest writing is a means for us to challenge and transform the objectified categories that people continually get put in – and the systems, standards, and regulations that frame, attempt to constrain, the stories that get told. Yes, genres, any genre – think hip hop, punk, death metal, fantasy, horror, romance – come with socially shared expectations and stylistic criteria on structure, rhythm, content, and emotionality that can be useful. They tell us something both about who writes the story, what story is being told, and what is expected of a story's audience. And any language we try to reinvent will be formed from languages of oppression that we already have. But as Will suggests, we can use the expectations and stylistic features that genre provides and play with them, subvert them, manipulate them, and imbue them with the forms of affect that we want these templates to vehiculate. And as Sibo argues, breaking disruptive categories and lenses requires us to challenge the language at our disposal. Experimenting with the syntax, style, vocabulary, and the very meanings of words, and utilising and producing knowledge in the form of poetry, music, and literature rather than only academic work as McKittrick (2021) suggests, allows us to challenge and resist the complex yet established and normalised linguistic system, which has long served the hegemony of rational science, capitalist means of production, and colonial violence (Isoke,

2018; McKittrick, 2021). While we admit that this Element is still written in fairly standard English – we have only begun this project – we are convinced that reimagining and reconstituting our present and our future requires us to invent and practise a new language, new genres, which in turn enable us to provoke new affects and agitations, to disrupt the socially shared narratives about how inequalities come into being, and paint another picture of how we want the world to be.

The third way in which we hope to enact banal resistance through our writing is by using it to locate places to make change. If inequalities are made through banal practices, then, we argue, these banal practices should be the starting point for their unmaking and transformation. As Hannah suggests, this could just be by being more flexible when someone is late for an appointment, or as little as taking a poster down from the wall. It is to be conscious of our often unconscious habits, and change the power relations we enact in the world. Even silence, which is so often paired with the complicit bystander, can at times resist rather than aid the production of inequalities. Of course, the world is complex, and people only have so much energy to give – our actions can never be perfect, and there are often trade-offs to be made, sides to be taken. But this is another reason to write. Writing is a process, a practice which can help us think about all our other practices. Our stories, and indeed the very practice of writing, allow us to unpack the complexities, lay them out on the page, a line to highlight, a corner to fold down, until we can locate the specific places, times, and relations in which inequality is constituted. It is only then that we can situate and negotiate places to take action, and change the stories we can come to tell.

To be clear, although we focus on the microphysical, banal resistance cannot be individualised and responsibilised; it needs to include everyone, everything, and be focused on how we choose to relate to one another. From Hannah's work (Cowan, 2021), it is clear that there are already people – such as healthcare workers who insist on breaking the protocol to get someone the care they need – that already use their banal actions to make change. Banal resistance too often comes from those who experience oppression themselves, and particularly from those who are oppressed by the feminisation of emotional and care labour. We want to be clear that banal resistance is hard work; it takes a material, physical, and mental toll, and at times those who resist have to deal with the fact that they get things wrong in a complex world. So writing about banal resistance is also a way to ensure that the labour of banal resistance can be better distributed; that our advocacy of banal resistance doesn't inadvertently reproduce labour inequalities. One way in which we, as writers and social scientists, could help here is to document banal practices which resist oppression (rather than only critique those that reproduce inequality), so that they can be recognised, discussed, and multiplied. Through writing, we can firstly make banal resistance, protest, action more accessible by making it visible, tangible, touchable, doable; or we could even normalise, legitimise, other ways of acting, of being in the world. But secondly, we suggest that writing can be a way to collectivse, to commonise the fight and ensure those who need it have downtime while their examples are shared. Here we suggest it may be useful to draw from lingual practices being developed in Disability Justice Theory – to openly speak about and distribute the 'spoons' or energy that people have to fight. At present, this is just a proposal, a plan; there is still more work to be done. But perhaps, if our banal actions can produce things as horrific as genocide, banal resistance could bring about spectacular disruption.

So then, we have identified these ways in which our writing can disrupt. But we are aware that our choices, our affects, the places we locate for banal resistance may not necessarily be shared by all those who read our texts. Indeed, at times we as editors disagree about the extent to which any of these mechanisms can make change (Alfonso, more wary of reproducing inequalities when we attempt to make change, and Hannah more wary of reproducing inequalities by doing nothing at all). In academia and beyond, after the text is finished, we are meant to become anxious about how to get our stories out there in the world; how can they be circulated and heard? But here the point of writing for us is not only for so many others to read it, and it is certainly not to instruct others about the world. Rather, writing, we argue, is more a form of exchange, of sharing ideas, which are not simply static finalised pieces there to be passively consumed. Written words must be spoken back to. This is another reason we argue that writing needs to be a more collective process; it is why we have attempted with this Element and our blog to bring writing to the commons. We intend to proliferate and expand forms of writing so that it cannot possibly all be held in the national libraries, in a neatly ordered systematic set of shelves or hidden away in vaults; a carefully created reading list, providing legitimised histories. To be clear, we are not advocating a process of democratisation, where one idea must win out against another in popular demand (Graeber, 2004). Rather, we want to multiply the stories that get told, and we especially want people to be able to write about their oppression (who are often in minorities) – because it is those who are most disrupted by unequal relations of power that have the best knowledge on how this power operates (Bloch & Adorno, 1988).

We realise our complicities and contradictions here. In the very writing of this Element we are partaking in, and benefitting from, the publishing industry that we critique in the very lines it has allowed us to write. The publishing industry in which we are engaging upholds the linguistic standards that we suggest we need to disrupt, and carefully selects writers which conform to the academic genre. We are aware that this publishing industry has historically contributed to the circulation and normalisation of oppressive knowledge subjecting people to forms of control and domination (Cusicanqui, 2019). And we are aware that there is a danger that publishing houses simply absorb forms of counter-knowledge, alternative stories about society, and contain this subversive knowledge as safely packaged commodities. For us, the decision to publish within this network of powerful relations is one we see as part of our own banal resistance. We intend to utilise and appropriate the powerful logistical forces which have enabled us to produce this volume at relatively low cost; their marketing infrastructures to create alliances and/or agitate audiences that we would not otherwise be able to reach; and the authority, which while corrupted and in need of contestation, imbues our stories with a form of power and legitimacy that can also be recognised by those who might most need to understand the way in which their actions produce banal inequalities. This banal resistance, we understand as a form of stealing, or theft, if you like. As a way of occupying space that others could occupy (potentially with more conformist stories), and using this space to disrupt and attempt to transform the relations of power we have observed. It goes without saying that this stealing does not solve the contradiction in which we find ourselves. But for us it is a first attempt, a first step, to navigate the complex relations of banal inequality, and claim back a system of knowledge production which has been stolen from us.

Again, we realise not everyone will agree, but that is the point. We want people to disagree. For us, this Element is supposed to be a launchpad for further discussion; it is just a beginning. And of course, the story is never finished. Writing provides an account that allows people to engage in a dialogue with others whose accounts may diverge from what is printed on the page. The story is there to be reworked, redrafted, in a multitude of ways by its readers who can come to their own conclusions for action. Because no story can relate directly to any other; it must be translated, sculpted to people's own lives. These ways of acting cannot merely be moved from one place to another without being malleated. Writing is also just a screenshot of a social world which is constantly in flux. Our conclusions must therefore be momentary, because each person we meet, every situation we experience and collaboration we make, stimulates a redraft, a reconsideration of our previously decisive stimulus for action. But writing, and rewriting, helps to contemplate and play out these potential actions, negotiate moments of change. It allows people to provoke new debates, and join older ones. It allows people to engage in unexpected conversations and alliances with actors who have already engaged in similar or different struggles. Writing is a form of connection, of figuring out how to realign relations in the world, and exchanging techniques and tactics to do so.

Writing banal inequalities, and fabricating stories which disrupt, is therefore an inherently collective process. This is not to say everyone has to literally write down their words on a page if they don't want to, and we are certainly not advocating for people to learn the styles and customs of academic writing in which we as editors are habituated. We want to embrace different methods, genres, and styles that we as editors are unaccustomed to. The collective nature of writing can emerge through spoken word, music, exchanges on messaging or content sharing apps, or scribbles from a permanent marker on the public toilet door. It also emerges through the people, things, scenarios, and conversations that have provoked these texts to be written. And finally, it emerges through readership, feedback, and contestations. Building on Caffentzis and Federici (2014) and bringing writing to the commons, we propose, could be one way to begin what Graeber (2004) would call a politics based on consensus. This means making space for people to converse through the commons in ways that multiply the voices that are heard and considered, rather than homogenise, categorise, and dominate them. It could be a way to collectively consider methods of banal resistance, for banal inequality affects everyone. And thinking with banal inequalities could allow people to share words which locate at least some power in everyday actions and relations with others. To think through and ricochet ideas together, in the knowledge that, collectively, our small lives contribute to the world we live with. But importantly, we want to learn from others. In other words, this Element is not the endpoint of a process, but rather a further step for us in a never-ending process of struggling for a different world.

References

Abu Lughod, L. (2008). Writing against culture. In T. Oakes & P. Price, eds., *The Cultural Geography Reader*. London: Routledge, pp. 466–79.

Adams, T. E., Jones, S. H., & Ellis, C. (2014). *Autoethnography: Understanding Qualitative Research*. Oxford: Oxford University Press.

Adichie, C. N. (2009). *The Danger of a Single Story* [video]. TEDGlobal. Available at: www.ted.com/talks/chimamanda_ngozi_adichie_the_danger_of_a_single_story/c.

Ahmed, S. (2000). *Strange Encounters: Embodied Others in Post-Coloniality*. London: Routledge.

Alexander, E. (2007). *Power and Possibility: Essays, Reviews, and Interviews*. Ann Arbor: University of Michigan Press.

Arendt, H. (1951). *The Origins of Totalitarianism*. Cleveland: Meridian Books.

Arendt, H. (1963). *Eichmann in Jerusalem: A Report on the Banality of Evil*. New York: Viking Press.

Bauman, R. & Briggs, C. (2002). Genre, intertextuality, and power. *Journal of Linguistic Anthropology*, 2(2), 131–72.

Bauman, R. & Briggs, C. (2004). *Voices of Modernity*. Cambridge: Cambridge University Press.

Bell, K. & Green, J. (2016). On the perils of invoking neoliberalism in public health critique. *Critical Public Health*, 26(3), 239–43. https://doi.org/10.1080/09581596.2016.1144872.

Berlant, L. (2015). The commons: Infrastructures for troubling times. *Environment and Planning D: Society and Space*, 34(3), 393–419. https://doi.org/10.1177%2F0263775816645989.

Billig, M. (1995). *Banal Nationalism*. London: Sage Publications.

Bloch, E. & Adorno, T. W. (1988). Something's missing: A discussion between Ernst Bloch and Theodor W. Adorno on the contradictions of utopian longing. In J. Zipes & F. Mecklenburg, trans. /eds., *The Utopian Function of Art and Literature: Selected Essays*. Studies in Contemporary German Social Thought. Cambridge, MA: MIT Press, pp. 1–17.

Bourdieu, P. (1984). *Distinction: A Social Critique of the Judgment of Taste*. Cambridge, MA: Harvard University Press.

Bourdieu, P. (2007). *Sketch for a Self-Analysis*. Cambridge: Polity Press.

Brenman, N. F. (2019). *Place, Need and Precarity in UK Mental Health Care: An Ethnography of Access*. London: The London School of Hygiene and Tropical Medicine. https://doi.org/10.17037/PUBS.04654391.

Brenman, N. F. (2020). Placing precarity: Access and belonging in the shifting landscape of UK mental health care. *Culture, Medicine, and Psychiatry*, 45, 22–41. https://doi.org/10.1007/s11013-020-09683-5.

Browning, C. (1992). *Ordinary Men: Reserve Police Batallion 101 and The Final Solution in Poland*. New York: HarperCollins.

Caffentzis, G. & Federici, S. (2014). Commons against and beyond capitalism. *Community Development Journal*, 49 (suppl. 1), i92–i105.

Callon, M. (1998). Introduction: The embeddedness of economic markets in economics. In M. Callon, ed., *The Laws of the Markets*. Oxford: Blackwell Publishers, pp. 1–58.

Campbell. J. (1949). *The Hero with a Thousand Faces*. New York: Pantheon Books.

Camus, A. (1961). *Resistance, Rebellion, and Death*. New York: Alfred A. Knopf

Césaire, A. (1945). Poésie et connaissance. *Tropiques*, 12, 157–70.

Césaire, A. (1950). *Discourse on Colonialism*. New York: Monthly Review Press.

Cowan, H. (2021). Taking the National(ism) out of the National Health Service: Re-locating agency to amongst ourselves. *Critical Public Health*, 31(2), 134–43. https://doi.org/10.1080/09581596.2020.1836328.

Crenshaw, K. (2015). Why intersectionality can't wait. *Washington Post*. Available at: www.washingtonpost.com/news/in-theory/wp/2015/09/24/why-intersectionality-cant-wait/.

Cusicanqui, S. R. (2019). Ch'ixinakax utxiwa: A reflection on the practices and discourses of decolonization. *Language, Culture, and Society*, 1(1), 106–19. https://doi.org/10.1075/lcs.00006.riv.

Dahlgreen, G. & Whitehead, M. (1991). *European Strategies for Tackling Social Inequities in Health: Levelling Up Part 2*. WHOLIS E89384. Copenhagen: World Health Organization.

Deleuze, G. & Guattari, F. (1987). *A Thousand Plateaus: Capitalism and Schizophrenia*. Minneapolis: University of Minnesota Press.

Douglas, M. (1966). *Purity and Danger: An Analysis of Concepts of Pollution and Taboo*. London: Routledge.

Fanon, F. (1952). *Black Skin, White Masks*. London: Pluto Press.

Fisher, M. (2009). *Capitalist Realism: Is There No Alternative?* Winchester: Zero Books.

Fitzgerald, D. & Callard, F. (2016). Entangling the medical humanities. In A. Whitehead, A. Woods, S. Atkinson, J. Macnaughton & J. Richards, eds., *The Edinburgh Companion to the Critical Medical Humanities*. Edinburgh: Edinburgh University Press, pp. 35–49.

Freire, P. (1970). *Pedagogy of the Oppressed*. New York: The Continuum Publishing Company.

Gilroy, P. (2001). *Against Race: Imagining Political Culture Beyond the Color Line*. Cambridge, MA: Belknap Press of Harvard University Press.

Glissant, É. (1997). *Poetics of Relation*. Ann Arbor: University of Michigan Press.

Graeber, D. (2004). *Fragments of an Anarchist Anthropology*. Chicago: Prickly Paradigm Press.

Gramsci, A. (1971). *Selections from the Prison Books*. New York: International Publishers.

Haraway, D. J. (2016). *Staying with the Trouble: Making Kin in the Chthulucene*. Durham, NC: Duke University Press.

Heller, M. & McElhinny, B. (2017). *Language, Capitalism, and Colonialism*. Toronto: University of Toronto Press.

Isoke, Z. (2018). Black ethnography, black(female)aesthetics: Thinking/writing/saying/sounding black political life. *Theory & Event*, 21(1), 148–68.

Kanafani, G. (2013[1968]). *Palestinian Literature of Resistance under Occupation 1948–1968*. Cyprus: Rimel Publications.

Lakshmi Piepzna-Samarasinha, L. (2018). *Care Work: Dreaming Disability Justice*. Vancouver: Arsenal Pulp Press.

Latour, B. (2005). *Reassembling the Social: An Introduction to Actor–Network Theory*. New York: Oxford University Press.

Law, J. (2004). *After Method: Mess in Social Science Research*. London: Routledge.

Law, J. & Lien, M. (2012). Slippery: Field notes on empirical ontology. *Social Studies of Science*, 43(3), 363–78. https://doi.org/10.1177%2F0306312712456947.

Levitas, R. (2013). *Utopia as Method: The Imaginary Reconstitution of Society*. London: Palgrave Macmillan.

McKittrick, K. (ed.) (2015). *Sylvia Wynter: On Being Human as Praxis*. Durham, NC: Duke University Press.

McKittrick, K. (2021). *Dear Science and Other Stories*. Durham, NC: Duke University Press.

Mehan, H., Hertweck, A., & Lee Meihls, J. (1986). *Handicapping the Handicapped*. Stanford: Stanford University Press.

Micheal, M. (2012). Anecdote. In C. Lury & N. Wakeford, eds., *Inventive Methods: The Happening of the Social*. London: Routledge, pp. 25–36.

Moten, F. (2003). *In the Break: The Aesthetics of the Black Radical Tradition*. Minneapolis: University of Minnesota Press.

Narayan, B. (2021). *Republic of Hindutva*. [S.l.]: Penguin Random House India.

Pandey, V. (2020). Bilkis Bano, 82, holds the portrait of DR B.R Ambedkar, during a sit in protest led by women, at Shaheen Bagh in New Delhi against new citizenship law. Permission gained. Available at: https://m.facebook.com/vijaypandeyphotography/photos/a.813408778808072/1504009813081295/.

Rascal. D. (2003). *Boy in da Corner* [music]. XL Recordings.

Roy, A. (1999). *The Cost of Living*. New York: HarperCollins.

Said, E. (1984). The future of criticism. *Modern Language Notes*, 99(4), 951–8. https://doi.org/10.2307/2905511.

The Clash. (1977). *White Riot* [music]. CBS Records International.

The Cosmopolitan of Las Vegas. (2010). Erislandy Lara vs. Carlos Molina at Fight Night at The Cosmopolitan of Las Vegas [photograph]. Licensed under CC BY-ND 2.0. Available at: www.flickr.com/photos/49869980@N07/5564962877.

Wacquant. L. (2006). *Body & Soul: Notebooks of an Apprentice Boxer*. New York: Oxford University Press.

Wakeford, N. & Lury, C. (2012). Introduction: A perpetual inventory. In N. Wakeford & C. Lury, eds., *Inventive Methods*. London: Routledge, pp. 1–25.

Wallace, D. (2018). Fred Moten's radical critique of the present. *New Yorker*, 30 April 2018, sec. Persons of Interest. Available at: www.newyorker.com/culture/persons-of-interest/fred-motens-radical-critique-of-the-present.

Wonker. (2010). *Vanilla Ice* [photograph]. Licensed under CC BY 2.0. Available at: www.flickr.com/photos/94056408@N00/4742513195.

Contributors

Natassia Brenman is a social scientist at the University of Oxford, currently researching technologies for remote healthcare and digital in/exclusion. Her PhD, completed in 2019 at the London School of Hygiene and Tropical Medicine, was an ethnography of access in inner city mental health services in London. She is interested in how health is shaped by social and material environments, and how this might generate new ways of thinking about and doing care.

Hannah Cowan is a medical sociologist/anthropologist working at the School of Life Course and Population Sciences, King's College London. She is interested in activism, social inequalities, and health. After completing her PhD on health inequalities at the London School of Hygiene and Tropical Medicine, she now works to bring non-academic communities and researchers together to help remake the world in which we live and find everyday ways of resisting the reproduction of inequalities.

Sibo Kanobana is Assistant Professor in Cultural Studies at the Open University of the Netherlands. His research explores how cultural and linguistic practices reproduce and challenge structural racism and coloniality. He's currently writing a book on whiteness and is co-editing a volume entitled *Subverting Space and Race* for the Critical Sociology of Language series (De Gruyter Mouton).

Amal Latif is a doctoral scholar in social anthropology based in India, researching gender and migration. Her research deals with the narratives of Indian migrant women domestic workers in the Gulf. Her other interests include shifting lines of minority politics and resistance in the contemporary Indian context.

Alfonso Del Percio is Associate Professor of Applied Linguistics. His research deals with the intersection of language, migration, and governmentality, and the links between language, work, and social inequality. Alfonso is co-editor of the journal *Language, Culture and Society*, and is currently working on a single-authored book entitled *Genealogies of State Propaganda*.

Will Nyerere Plastow is a writer and filmmaker based in Manchester. He has extensive experience working in both factual and drama television. His play *Terror Management Theory* was performed by the UK's leading black theatre company as part of the 2021 Talawa Firsts Festival. He has also co-directed a documentary, *Sunset at Dawn*, which shone a light on poor public maternity care in Kenya.

Cambridge Elements ≡

Applied Linguistics

Li Wei

University College London

Li Wei is Chair of Applied Linguistics at the UCL Institute of Education, University College London (UCL), and Fellow of Academy of Social Sciences, UK. His research covers different aspects of bilingualism and multilingualism. He was the founding editor of the following journals: *International Journal of Bilingualism* (Sage), *Applied Linguistics Review* (De Gruyter), *Language, Culture and Society* (Benjamins), *Chinese Language and Discourse* (Benjamins) and *Global Chinese* (De Gruyter), and is currently Editor of the *International Journal of Bilingual Education and Bilingualism* (Taylor and Francis). His books include the *Blackwell Guide to Research Methods in Bilingualism and Multilingualism* (with Melissa Moyer) and *Translanguaging: Language, Bilingualism and Education* (with Ofelia Garcia) which won the British Association of Applied Linguistics Book Prize.

Zhu Hua

University College London

Zhu Hua is Professor of Language Learning and Intercultural Communication at the UCL Institute of Education, University College London (UCL) and is a Fellow of Academy of Social Sciences, UK. Her research is centred around multilingual and intercultural communication. She has also studied child language development and language learning. She is book series co-editor for *Routledge Studies in Language and Intercultural Communication* and *Cambridge Key Topics in Applied Linguistics*, and Forum and Book Reviews Editor of *Applied Linguistics* (Oxford University Press).

About the Series

Mirroring the *Cambridge Key Topics in Applied Linguistics*, this Elements series focuses on the key topics, concepts and methods in Applied Linguistics today. It revisits core conceptual and methodological issues in different subareas of Applied Linguistics. It also explores new emerging themes and topics. All topics are examined in connection with real-world issues and the broader political, economic and ideological contexts.

Cambridge Elements ≡

Applied Linguistics

Printed in the United States
by Baker & Taylor Publisher Services